A
DANCE
AUTOBIOGRAPHY

A DANCE AUTOBIOGRAPHY BY NATALIA MAKAROVA

INTRODUCED AND EDITED BY

GENNADY SMAKOV

PHOTOGRAPHS BY

DINA MAKAROVA AND OTHERS

ALFRED A. KNOPF

NEW YORK 1979

01148

THIS IS A BORZOI BOOK
PUBLISHED BY ALFRED A. KNOPF, INC.
COPYRIGHT © 1979 BY NATALIA MAKAROVA KARKAR

LIBRARY OF CONGRESS CATALOGING IN PUBLICATION DATA
MAKAROVA, NATALIA, [DATE]   A DANCE AUTOBIOGRAPHY.
1.   MAKAROVA, NATALIA, [DATE]   2.   DANCERS—RUSSIA—BIOGRAPHY.
I.   SMAKOV, GENNADY GRIGOR'EVICH.   II.   MAKAROVA, DINA.   III.   TITLE.
GV1785.M26A35   1979   792.8'092'4 [B]   78-20621   ISBN 0-394-50141-1

MANUFACTURED IN THE UNITED STATES OF AMERICA
FIRST EDITION

TO MY SON, ANDRUSHA

CONTENTS

ACKNOWLEDGMENTS
9

INTRODUCTION
12

BECOMING A BALLERINA
15

DANCING IN RUSSIA
39

DANCING IN THE WEST
83

EPILOGUE
167

PHOTOGRAPHIC PLATES
177

PHOTOGRAPHIC CREDITS

Page 46, Wayne J. Shilkert. 58, bottom right, Jennie Walton. 59, top right, Walton; bottom, Nina Alavert. 62, 63, 66, Walton. 67, Rosemary Winckley. 70, top left, Victor Welch; bottom left, Walton. 71, top left, Winckley; bottom, Walton. 74, top, Winckley. 75, bottom right, Alavert. 79, bottom left and right, Walton. 83, Kenn Duncan. 86, top right, Zoë Dominic; bottom, Walton. 95, top left and bottom right, Martha Swope; bottom left and top right, Dina Makarova. 99, 107, 114–15, D. Makarova. 122, top left, Louis Péres; bottom left, D. Makarova; bottom right, Swope. 126–7, Dominic. 130, top left and bottom, Lois Greenfield; top right, D. Makarova. 135, top left, D. Makarova; bottom left, Walton; right, Mira. 138–9, D. Makarova. 143, top left and bottom right, D. Makarova; bottom left, Edward Griffiths; top right, Leslie E. Spatt. 146, 150, 155, D. Makarova. 159, bottom right, D. Makarova; all others, Swope. 162, top left and right, D. Makarova; bottom, Max Waldman. 167, Duncan. 171, 174–5, D. Makarova. 177, Duncan. 179, Mike Humphrey. 180, Mira. 181–5, D. Makarova. 186, Spatt. 187, D. Makarova. 188, Walton. 189, Spatt. 190–1, D. Makarova. 192, Swope. 193, Beverley Gallegos. 195, Waldman. 196, Swope. 197, D. Makarova. 198–9, Fred Fehl. 200, Anthony Crickmay. 201, Spatt. 202, Swope. 203, D. Makarova. 204–5, Swope. 206, Mira. 207, Crickmay. 209, D. Makarova. 210, Swope. 211, D. Makarova. 212, top, D. Makarova; bottom, Fehl. 213, top, D. Makarova; bottom, Fehl. 214, Swope. 215, D. Makarova. 216–17, Swope. 218, D. Makarova. 219, Costas. 220–1, D. Makarova. 222, Swope. 223-4, D. Makarova. 225, Péres. 227, Swope. 228–9, Bliokh. 230-3, Spatt. 234, Judy Cameron. 235, 237, D. Makarova. 238, Fehl. 239, D. Makarova. 240-1, Cameron. 242, Eric Feinblatt. 243, D. Makarova. 244, Mira. 245, Crickmay. 246-7, D. Makarova. 248, Crickmay. 249, D. Makarova. 250–1, Crickmay. 252, D. Makarova. 253, Crickmay. 254-6, D. Makarova. 257, top, Fehl; bottom, D. Makarova. 258, Crickmay. 259, Duncan. 260-2, D. Makarova. 263-4, Swope. 265-6, D. Makarova. 267, Jack Vartoogian. 268, D. Makarova. 269, 271–5, Swope. 276–7, D. Makarova. 278, Swope. 280, Bliokh. 281, D. Makarova. 282-3, Duncan. 284-5, Swope. 288, D. Makarova. 289, Fehl. 290–2, D. Makarova. 293, Sue Martin. 295, Waldman. 296–7, Walton. 298–9, D. Makarova. 300–1, Swope. 302–3, Walton. 304–6, Swope. 307, Walton. 308–9, Waldman. 310, Walton. 311, D. Makarova. 313, Seth Eastman Moebs. 316–17, Patricia Barnes. 318, Walton. 319, Barnes. 320, Cameron. 321, Swope. 322–31, D. Makarova. 332-3, Cameron. 334–6, D. Makarova. 337, Gallegos. 338–9, Swope. 340-1, D. Makarova. 342, Cameron. 343, D. Makarova. 344, Humphrey. 345, Spatt. 346–7, D. Makarova. 349, Frederika Davis. 352-3, Walton. 354, Swope. 355, Mira. 356, D. Makarova. 357, Sabine Toepffer. 358, D. Makarova. 359–60, Mira. 361–6, D. Makarova. We would like to express our gratitude to Soviet photographers, whom unfortunately we have been unable to identify, for photographs that appear on the following pages: 15, 26, 30, 39, 43, 47, 51, 55, 58, 59, 70, 71, 74, 75, 79, 86, 122, 314–15, 350–1.

ACKNOWLEDGMENTS

Before acknowledging the specific people who have so generously aided me with this book, I must thank those without whom there would have been no career to record in its pages: the Kirov School, for giving me an education, a culture, a foundation for everything I may have accomplished; the Kirov Theatre, for polishing my work and making me into a ballerina; and all my teachers, coaches, and colleagues in both school and theatre, especially Natalia Dudinskaya, Konstantin Sergeyev, and Tatiana Vecheslova. It is my hope that my work since 1970, as they may infer it from this book, will not seem unworthy of them.

It gives me great pleasure to thank the following people who gave their time and effort to helping me with this book.

First of all, my husband Edward, for his encouragement and advice, and Genna Smakov, for all his patience and perception in working with me on the text. Then to my friend of many years, Dina Makarova, who has given me so much help and support, as well as practically documenting my life on stage and off through the years since I left the Kirov. Dina also helped tremendously in gathering the photographic material from the other photographers represented in this book. And I want to thank all of those photographers for their cooperation—without them, of course, this kind of record of an artist's career would not be possible. Others who helped in the gathering of the pictures were Helen and Sheldon Atlas, Rosemary Winckley, and Patricia Barnes; and Charles France of American Ballet Theatre was of great importance in helping to choose and prepare the photographs and in advising on the overall aesthetic of the book. My thanks also to Elena Tchernishova, for her help in recollecting so many aspects of my early work.

Finally, I must thank those at Knopf who have worked so hard to create this book: Bob Scudellari, who is responsible for the design; Ellen McNeilly, who not only oversaw the production of the book, but herself printed many of the photographs from negatives; Neal Jones and Ellen Mastromonaco, the production editors; Martha Kaplan and Karen Latuchie; and first and foremost Bob Gottlieb, my editor, for everything.

A
DANCE
AUTOBIOGRAPHY

This book has been worked on in New York, San Francisco, Washington, D.C., Baltimore, and Philadelphia. It grew like a snowball out of dozens of taped interviews and informal conversations with Natalia Makarova. Most often we talked after performances or rehearsals, which would inevitably give us fresh material for discussion. Later I "processed" the tapes, and these pages contain the essence of the miles of tapes that accumulated over more than two years.

I had known Natalia Makarova since her debut at the Kirov and had always believed that her unique and precious gift was unpredictable in its manifestations, that her naturally spontaneous expression was incompatible with preliminary rational calculations or analytical control. Our very first talk about *Giselle* in the summer of 1976 upset all my conceptions about her. With great passion she told me of her incessant work on the familiar role of the peasant girl, how, every time before going out on stage, she imagined her character in a slightly different way, how she deliberately changed accents every time she danced Giselle. I was astonished: behind the apparent spontaneity I found a true artist's laboratory with a rich choice of test tubes and jars from which she would, at each performance, create new combinations, prompted by her inspiration.

From the very beginning, Makarova wanted to talk about ballet theory, and sometimes, like a possessed mountain climber, she reached such heights that neither of us could find a way back to earth. In her emotional and inquisitive way she wanted to discover clear definitions for everything, she wanted to define the difference between romantic, classical, and neo-classical ballet, the difference between Russian and Western dancing schools, and so on. Sometimes, as I came close to drowning in this flood of words, I felt that my formerly firm ideas about the ballet were on the verge of being shattered.

She was passionate and persistent in her judgments, and I had to summon all the authorities to my defense—from Noverre to Edwin Denby. She dismissed all the accepted opinions. For the first time in her life she had the opportunity to speak at length, and she rushed forward, without picking her way. Sometimes when she lacked words, she substituted a pantomime or a dance. Her ideas were not always well formulated: like many dancers, she was embarrassed by an imagined inarticulateness. The necessary precision of words often seemed to her inadequate to express the vast variety of sensations and illuminations that, like lightning, struck her mind after each performance or were born as a response to my questions, and to her whole dancing experience.

When, together, we tried to shape her sensations into words, she was most often dissatisfied, saying: "It's trivial . . . uninteresting . . . nonsense. . . ." But she liked the process of reflection and emotional talking out: for the first time after all these years filled with dancing, she listened to her own words, saw them written down on paper, and slowly accustomed herself to the limitations of verbal expression.

Step by step, the work on the book became indispensable to her; not unlike psychoanalytical sessions, it turned into a conscious search for her own identity, in a form that was entirely new to her. Her actual biography seemed uninteresting to her ("Who wants to know all these banal details?")—she was ruthless in deleting everything that was not directly related to the art of dance. From session to session my role varied from that of a compassionate listener to that of an adversary in a fierce argument, with the two of us, in good Russian tradition, screaming at each other. Soon she felt I alone was no longer enough for her, she decided to widen the audience, and our interviews turned into unique ballet seminars. On different occasions, among the participants were our friends in common and Makarova's colleagues from the Kirov and the Royal Ballet: Mikhail Baryshnikov, Alexander Minz, Georgina Parkinson, and, in particular, Elena Tchernishova, whose analytical gifts—those of an experienced coach and teacher—brought clarity and precision to our arguments. I want to express my gratitude to all of these, as well as to all the others who helped and encouraged us in our work: Suzanne Massie, Dina Makarova, Helen and Sheldon Atlas, Eugenia and Henri Doll, and of course Makarova's husband, Edward Karkar.

The first draft of the book was finished early in the winter of 1977. Makarova had lots of free time then—she was expecting a baby, and we secluded ourselves in her San Francisco house to work on the manuscript. After she had read it all, she said to my horror: "All right, now it's time to start working: that is merely a first draft." We worked for another month. When, as I thought, we had done all that we could, the revised manuscript was given over to our kind and knowledgeable editor, Robert Gottlieb. He "brushed it up" and then, with his characteristic professionalism and attention to detail, asked us to enlarge the theoretical passages. The book started growing again. It took six more months of intense work. Makarova was different now: she had learned to comprehend her subtle sensations that earlier had been too elusive to put into words. She tried as much as she could to restrain her obsessiveness, understanding that it is impossible to say everything in one book, and yet, having re-read the final version of the book, she said: "Well, now it looks almost decent, but, strictly speaking, we should have worked on it for at least another year."

In this phrase I recognized the true Makarova: the perfectionist. She does not accept any compromise, for herself or for others. She is never content with today's ballet, but tries to see its tomorrow. When the work of creation is over, it is no longer interesting to her. And so today she feels that this book of her thoughts and reflections on classical dance is only the first step toward the ideal "last and final" confession that, I hope, one day she will write.

—Gennady Smakov

BECOMING
A BALLERINA

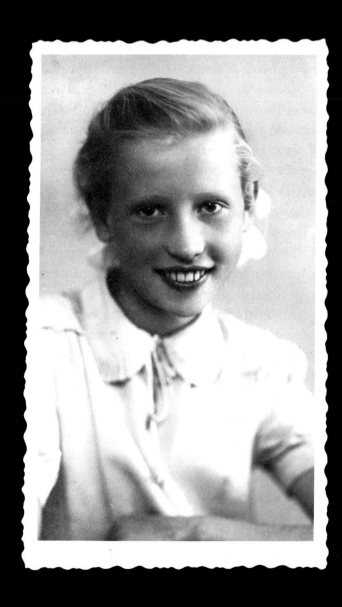

a gymnastics group, but I ended up in ballet; I honestly don't remember why. I only remember feeling somehow perplexed, oppressed, ashamed, that I was an ugly duckling among swans—from childhood I had considered myself unattractive, and can't overcome that complex even now, no matter what anyone may say. Pretty boys and girls were ceremoniously pacing through a polonaise, floating through a Russian dance, working on various positions. Completely at a loss, I wasn't able to stay in step. At home I broke into tears from the humiliation and the knowledge of my worthlessness. But I didn't drop out—probably because of the challenge, and a feeling of excitement, and the desire to assert myself in spite of everything and everyone. It was tortuous and difficult, and therefore I was totally engrossed. That feeling of challenge is very much with me still; for instance, sometimes I get much more satisfaction out of dancing *The Sleeping Beauty,* with its refined classical choreography, than I do from *Giselle,* whose romantic spirit runs in my blood, so to speak, and comes much easier for me. But all of this was as far away as the moon, then.

I did take part in an amateur production; we danced some crazy pieces, Snowflakes around the Christmas tree. On stage I not only managed to get my own movements mixed up but also to throw off all the others, so that the entire dance turned into a mess. I started howling right on stage. Then once—I really don't know which of my virtues evoked it—my teacher, Zinaida Ivanovna, said to me: "You'd be better off, Miss, over at the Vaganova School. Things will be more interesting for you there." I had never in my life even seen the place, but since I frequently wandered around the city on my own, I found Rossi Street without any difficulty. The announcement that applications were being accepted was terrifying. I don't know why it was that I walked in and asked where to apply—I suppose curiosity had the upper hand.

I went up to the third floor as I was told to do. At the top of the stairs, I could see a sign: "Medical Section." I remember thinking, "What for? I'm not sick," but I went in all the same. They put me on the scales and started to look me over. Then they telephoned somewhere, and a very fat gentleman appeared—he turned out to be the director of the school, Mr. Shelkov. He lifted up one of my legs à la seconde, then the other; at the time, my legs went off in various directions a lot better than they do now. I was terribly frightened, and when they asked for my telephone number I gave them the wrong one; thank goodness I didn't give them the wrong surname. To this day I don't know how they managed to find me later. I am indebted to Shelkov for a great deal; because of him I did not have to take an entrance examination. They weighed me, as it were, and took me into the School. I'm told that Shelkov, after my graduation recital, would console parents who were upset at the entrance of their children into the Vaganova School, by saying: "You never know what kind of ballerina your daughter will make. Natalia Makarova's parents were very opposed to her entering, and what a dancer she has become!" Though he would hardly dare to say that now, after my "defection." Shelkov's phone call really did create havoc at home, a real drama. My mother was horrified: how could I, the daughter of an engineer and granddaughter of an architect, an "heir to the intelligentsia," plan to spend my whole life hopping around on my toes? What sort of a profession was that? And I, who had forgotten all about my meeting with Shelkov, rebelled on the spot—from sheer stubbornness, of course; and the more I stamped my feet, screamed, and cried, the more entering the school became essential to me. It became an obsession, and my parents gave in.

I was pleased with my victory but, alas, not with what awaited me at school. For, from the first day, my schooling turned into hell. I was put into an experimental class, created for children born on the eve of World War II or during the war. This generation, to which I belonged, grew up through Russia's hungriest, most excruciating years. The children were so weak physically that they couldn't dream of ballet school, regardless of any artistic aspirations they might have. No wonder that right after the war— between 1945 and 1947—the Vaganova School could hardly fill its classrooms. No parents would allow their children to study there.

Usually children had entered at age nine or ten. I entered the Vaganova School at the age of thirteen. At the beginning of the fifties, the experimental class was introduced for especially gifted teen-agers of fourteen or fifteen who would not otherwise have got into the ballet. In this brand-new class the usual nine-year program was condensed into six years. Teen-agers had to continue their normal education in the Vaganova School and in addition complete the nine-year ballet curriculum in six years.

Our study took place at a wild, headlong pace. For example, they put us on pointe in the first year, whereas students usually had begun with toe shoes only in the second. Learning the grammar of classical ballet so quickly had its drawbacks: it hit us in too much of a rush. In our experimental class, running ahead like thoroughbred trotters, we somehow violated our physical equipment, because our bodies didn't have the time to develop the necessary muscles. One must learn not only with one's head, but even more with one's body, whose muscular memory is not so nimble as the mind's; it must be built up over years, so that the body, as a sensitive instrument, can react precisely. Just as a good pianist does not look at his fingers, a trained dancer should not think about technical devices of execution. Only then can he control his body so that it expresses what is in the heart, what comes from the soul. That was the goal of Vaganova's method, aiming at the gradual development of ballet technique based on the slow building up of all the muscles.

In other words, in our special class, the Vaganova method could not lead to such dazzling results as it usually did, and each of us suffered from this in his own way.

As for me, I had very soft legs by nature. Their muscles were elastic and flexible enough, which suited me ideally as a romantic ballerina, but they were rather weak to cope with the technique of Marius Petipa's ballets, which demand that a well-trained body perform their academic combinations almost automatically, with no effort at all. The muscles of my legs couldn't contract very fast, and developed very slowly; legs usually demand a more gradual and careful conditioning to add iron strength to their flexibility. Some schoolgirls in our experimental class had the dry and firm muscles that were very easy to strengthen over the years. My soft legs needed more than six years for strengthening, and I had to work on this problem through further years of training, even while performing on the stage of the Kirov.

Meanwhile, my legs were growing their muscles slowly, they were still soft, and that used to affect the consistency of my performance, especially in full-length ballets. My weak muscles would grow tired sooner than they were supposed to. I could, for instance, dance decently for one act, which would serve me as a warming up, do well in the second act, and fall apart in the third from plain physical fatigue.

Each school day was filled to the brim. What didn't we study! Besides the required middle-school program, we had our class for two hours a day, plus history of ballet, literature, history, music, art history, piano lessons, French. We learned traditional dances, character dancing, adagio, dramatic art, fencing (only for the boys); all this knowledge was suddenly dumped on our adolescent shoulders. In this intensive method there were many advantages: a lot of things from the humanities simply stuck in the mind. But the burden was absolutely crushing. The Vaganova School, practically speaking, combined three courses of study: the usual subjects, music, and ballet. I, and all the other pupils, arrived at school at eight in the morning and got home only around eight at night. When I was also busy with performances at the Theatre, I would reach home at eleven and have to start thinking about lessons for the next day when all I wanted to do was sleep. It was especially painful in the winter, when the days are so short, and I hardly saw the sun at all.

We used to run around all day like wind-up toys, and if you wanted to get something out of your academic courses (though many didn't), then you could simply go crazy. Because of my cursed perfectionism, I crammed day and night. I didn't understand a thing about physics or mathematics, and only some miracle kept me from breaking down. Fortunately, I lived only twenty minutes from school by trolley bus. Even now I vividly remember how I used to freeze at the bus stop waiting for my trolley, and how I prayed to God for its immediate appearance. "Wait just a little bit longer, it's coming, it's coming," I kept saying to myself, barely able to feel my fingers and toes that were almost numb from the ferocious cold. How often I would walk into the classroom with my extremities half frost-bitten! And then recovering in the warmth of indoors would cause unbearable pain. Many of my friends lived outside the city and, long before dawn, had to get up to take a commuter train, then transfer to a streetcar filled to overflowing. They would arrive with trampled feet, worn out even before they got into harness for the exhausting routine of the School.

The school building was five stories high, and every day I'd race up and down like a mad person, along with everybody else. (The elevator was reserved for teachers.) The normal program and the ballet program were not coordinated. Let's say you had literature the first hour, on the second floor; then with only a ten-minute break you would have to change on the fifth floor and get down to the third for classical ballet, always afraid of being late—the discipline in that regard was monastic. There would be no time even to think of warming up. Right after classical ballet you would have mathematics and, again with only ten minutes, you would have to fly to the changing room on the fifth—you'd never have time to take a shower—get dressed or, dazed, simply pull on your uniform over your tights and then sit in class and dry out and catch your breath and never have time to think.

Then came the lunch break, and you were faced with a dilemma: whether to get ready for the next lesson—let's say study a musical score or some French—or to eat and rest. It's true the food was horrible, cutlets composed mostly of bread, potato pancakes every day, macaroni, almost no meat. In the early fifties the whole country was subsisting on bread and water, since the economy had been torn apart by the war; there was no way to obtain delicacies. Moreover, the cook stole food shamelessly, and of the insignificant rations which the school was allowed to give us to keep up our strength, only crumbs came our way. Many years later, when I was already a principal dancer at the Kirov, I used to stop by the School canteen, and there was the same deplorable situation—the scanty food, the squalor, the bad service. I could only wonder from where those poor kids got the energy to cope with the superhuman burden of their work.

There is no other place like the Vaganova School; it is unique, because it is the direct continuation of Russian balletic culture. Thanks to Diaghilev's "Russian Seasons" in the West and to all who participated in them and then settled in Europe after the Revolution, the culture of the Russian ballet spread throughout the world and became that protoplasm from which the Western ballet grew. Having crossed the threshold of this school, you were immediately immersed in a special atmosphere, a somewhat old-fashioned and, at the same time, typically Russian atmosphere of life in the service of the arts, service that was to become the purpose of *your* life. It pushes everything personal, all day-to-day concerns, into the background— it becomes the pivotal point, the basis of your existence.

I was unbelievably lucky. In the early fifties the Vaganova School was still an oasis of Russian culture amidst fragments of former glory. The experiments of Vsevolod Meyerhold and Alexander Tairov in the theatre had already been trampled on and destroyed; their names were taboo even for serious students of Russian art and historians of the theatre. The dramatic theatres themselves, having been subjected to the militant dictates of Socialist Realism, stagnated in routine. After Sergei Eisenstein's death, only a pitiful echo remained of the grandeur of the Russian film. Literature was immobilized in the grip of vicious censorship, which made even Nicholas I's infamous Third Section look like a childish caprice. But the Vaganova School and the Kirov Theatre flowered, not yet touched by the general decay so apparent elsewhere in Leningrad, the cradle of three revolutions, whose iron traditions led to unremitting ideological control over the arts. Ballet, with its nymphs and princes and sleeping beauties, still remained a refuge only slightly disturbed by the iron boot of Socialist Realism. Certain things had been damaged, spoiled here and there, but nothing had been destroyed utterly. Ballet was hardly amenable to the Party's curbs, although certainly, there was the occasional work in which obsessed Soviet tractor drivers would dance (on pointe) their vexation at a bad harvest. But this had not yet become the daily reality of ballet.

They said that Stalin himself spared the classical ballet and that he was personally taken with the dancing of Marina Semyonova. Perhaps it was for this reason that his minions left this relic of the sybaritic Imperial times alone. Miraculously, Stalin's purges passed over our school's old teachers such as Nikolai Ivanovsky and Mikhail Mikhailov. Their roots went back to St. Petersburg, and they escaped the fate of millions who rotted in the camps of the Gulag. They were permitted to live and to work, passing on, with inspiration, the tradition of the St. Petersburg ballet, which many of them had known personally, for they had begun in the days of Petipa and Ivanov. And this spirit of the Russian literary and artistic world wafted through the School. It was felt not only in the teaching method set down and perfected by Agrippina Vaganova, once a soloist with the Imperial Ballet (a great teacher, she died in 1951, two years before I entered the school) but in the refined Petersburg speech of my tutors, in their manner of conducting a discussion, their dress, and so on. And to us, future Giselles, Auroras, and Albrechts, they served as living examples of social grace and elegant simplicity in manners. Most of them were graduates of exclusive schools for the Russian aristocracy, such as the Smolny Institute, and knew thoroughly not only their own subject but French and literature and painting as well. They had grey hair, knew much, and had wide experience, and I was in awe of them and thankful for the very fact of their existence.

Nikolai Ivanovich Ivanovsky, who treated me very kindly, always wore spats and patent leather shoes and would say "My respects" to us kids and doff his hat when he met us on the street. And this was a better lesson for us than any of the sermons on Communist morality we heard. Ivanovsky taught us traditional dances, and working with him turned into excursions to the France of the Sun King or Spain during the time of the Hapsburgs. He did not simply show us how to move in the gavotte or the pavane; to the movements themselves he supplied stories of the temper of those distant periods that inflamed our young imaginations no less than the novels of Dumas.

Thanks to people like Ivanovsky, on the Kirov stage there was an unusually high standard of gesture, without which there is no style—and the slightest carelessness in style or breach of good taste was criminal there.

And my teacher Mikhail Mikhailovich Mikhailov, himself nurtured by Andrianov and Kschessinsky (a brother of the prima ballerina assoluta Matilda Kschessinskaya, who had been the young Czarevitch's mistress), was an embodiment of such culture, his comments and advice were so precise and correct. He began his career in Petipa's time and between 1920 and the 1950's had danced a multitude of classical and character parts. Naturally, he had much to share with me, who had just arrived in the world of the theatre. I've always remembered his advice: "Each role in ballet begins with the walk. This is the natural physical movement according to Stanislavsky." Mikhailov told me: "Learn to walk like Juliet or Giselle, and then you'll find the key to their plastic movement, to infusing it with precise emotion. This will emerge when you find the proper, the true, natural inner state. The body and the soul will then be in equilibrium, and the role will 'fit' you like a well-made dress in which you are free and comfortable."

But what was I to do when my heroines hardly walked about the stage at all—for instance, Odette in *Swan Lake?* How to find the balance my teacher spoke of? The formula was the same. Find the inner state, incarnate it, but not as an actress—rather as a person—grab onto some feature in Odette: shyness, her regal dignity, her ability to forgive, and be happy in this. And all of the formal combination of sissonnes ouvertes en effacé, all the ronds de jambe in the adagio, will be filled with feeling and meaning. It would seem to be that simple, but in order to learn to do it properly, a whole lifetime may not be enough.

And how Mikhailov worked with me to teach me to run on stage! It is so difficult to accomplish; almost no one can do it properly. Almost everyone does it in a theatrical manner, so that there is nothing in the movement but convention and boredom. For me, a real ballerina begins with her ability to walk or run on stage. Actually, running on stage is one of the ways of appropriating space, of cutting through it with the body. And whether she does it with her whole being, whether she fills space with the energy of her individuality, whether she moves naturally or is merely acting, means everything to me. I shall never forget how Galina Ulanova as Juliet flew to her meeting with Romeo, the black wings of her cloak streaming out behind her. An observant eye could discern everything in this—the surge of passion, the willful rush toward future happiness, with the black cloak floating above like the threat of impending catastrophe.

The most significant thing about the Vaganova School was very likely the daily, unobtrusive feeling of contact with the great ballet of the past, its traditions and unwritten laws, which nourished us like mother's milk. You simply couldn't get away from it. I used to spend hours in the little museum in the school run by the efficient and hospitable Marietta Frangopolo. She had once studied with George Balanchine in this very place and was a walking encyclopedia of ballet. She would tell us about the former Maryinsky Theatre and show us pictures of Pavlova, Nijinsky, Karsavina, Semyonova, Ulanova. I felt their fascinating presence constantly. Entering a classroom, I could almost see their legendary figures gazing out at me from the mottled depths of the mirrors that reflected my every mistake. My idols were Anna Pavlova and Galina Ulanova. I knew both of them only from pictures. I first saw the films of Pavlova in London after my defection, and I could only then really appreciate her greatness, so different from that of Ulanova, whom I revered as a goddess of the dance. Pavlova astonished me with the beauty of her legs, the cantilena of her unusually expressive, inspired movements, which, however, were slightly tinged with decadence, a certain affectation characteristic of the first quarter of this century.

In photographs, Ulanova seemed to be quite a different dancer. I saw her a little later, in *Romeo and Juliet* only, and in the *Giselle* film made in London. In a strange way, her image did not strike me as that of a contemporary, though she was dancing just four hundred miles away in Moscow's Bolshoi Theatre. She seemed inextricably bound up with the past, for the inspired beauty of her dancing, the inexpressible poetry of her gestures, her slightest movement seemed quite unattainable in contemporary ballet. Many times since then, watching her on the screen, I have tried to discern the secret of the bewitching lyricism of her Giselle and, especially, her Juliet. Only one thing comes to mind—simplicity, the precious economy of expressive means, all of it emanating from the heart.

I could never forget her Juliet, nor—a silly memory—a curtain call at the Kirov. She had danced Juliet in a jubilee performance in honor of Gerbek, at the Kirov, in 1957–58. I don't remember how she danced, but I do remember her taking a bow in Juliet's cloak—and high-heeled winter boots! She was late for a train to Moscow and had been hurriedly dressed in the wings. These somewhat vulgar boots were so out of keeping with her Botticelli image, as if to emphasize the rift between the poetic illusion of ballet and boring everyday reality.

In my mature years, I have never tried to imitate Ulanova, although after my debut in *Giselle* and *Les Sylphides,* some people began calling me "a young Ulanova," to my chagrin. It was flattering, of course, but didn't really give me much pleasure. In Ulanova's great art there was something so uniquely hers that it could not be copied.

Over the years, my enchantment with Ulanova has not diminished in the slightest. Nevertheless, some of her performances have grown dim. Quite recently, I watched her entrance as Odette on film, and, however magical, it seemed a bit contrived to me. This might be because Ulanova was really an ideal romantic ballerina, absolutely unmatchable in *Giselle* and *Les Sylphides*; it was her genius for understatement and subtle shading that constituted the strongest side of her talent. She danced *Swan Lake* as a simple romantic fairy tale in accordance with the old romantic tradition, with no concern about it as a psychological drama, and the lyrical understatement that made itself felt in her plasticity was not sufficient to convey the full drama of Odette's image. Her Queen of Swans seemed to be uniformly colored. Odette might have been interpreted thusly by all the Maryinsky ballerinas, except perhaps for Pavlova, whose unique achievement did not leave any trace in Ulanova. As for Maya Plisetskaya's entrance as Odette, it was much more daring and dynamic, disregarding traditional interpretation. While her approach was grounded in Tchaikovsky's music, in a way she revised Petipa's style for the sake of more psychological depth, reflecting the psychological experience of her contemporaries. As ballerinas, Ulanova and Plisetskaya belonged to two different generations, and their artistic creeds manifested themselves clearly in this one specific moment: Odette's entrance in Act II.

The artistic microcosm of our school was a reflection of the macrocosm of the city of Leningrad, whose architectural forms truly embody the best in Russian culture. Even Rossi Street itself (formerly Theatre Street), with the harmony of its austerely classical yellow buildings, inevitably fostered a feeling of proportion, restraint, and beauty. The School was an integral part of the Kirov Theatre, whose stars rehearsed in our building, and one had only to cross the hall to catch sight of Dudinskaya, Shelest, Balabina, or Bregvadze at work. Each one of them had tremendous individuality of style and technique, and they seemed to us almost like divine beings.

The Vaganova School has changed—I am unable to do anything about the nostalgic tone that inevitably colors these lines. With the deaths of Shiriaev, Pushkin, Ivanovsky, Mikhailov, that atmosphere of artistry I had breathed has departed—along with their extraordinary standards of mastery and inspiration. Those of my old teachers who are still alive have gone into retirement. They were replaced by a generation of dancers older than I, and the continuity that Vaganova had sustained for decades was broken.

There were many reasons why the live thread of teaching tradition that had been handed down from one generation of teachers to another was now broken. In Vaganova's time, each teacher would take her group up to a cer-

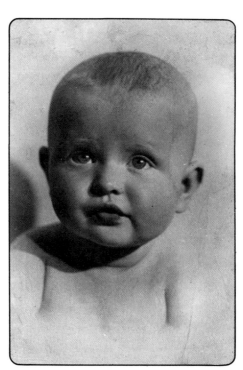

Right: At six months

Far right and below:
At fourteen

tain age and then turn it over to her successor: Snetkova-Vecheslova (her daughter Tatiana Vecheslova was later to become my coach) would teach the kids (nine- to twelve-year-olds); Romanova (Galina Ulanova's mother) was in charge of the intermediates; and as the girls grew up, she would hand them over to Vaganova for final polishing. Vaganova used to take the selection of faculty members very seriously. She believed that one had to be born a ballet teacher the way some are born poets or ballerinas. Often she would see a gifted teacher in a mediocre dancer, such as Tyuntina and Elena Shiripina. And she never made a mistake. Her pupils shared a common Vaganova method of teaching. They all had the same training; they were all operating from the same theoretical foundation.

In the fifties the old guard of teachers, undeviating in their worship of Petersburg ballet traditions, died out. They were replaced by Natalia Dudinskaya, Tyuntina, Shiripina, and several others of Vaganova's students who inherited all that was best from their own teacher. Tyuntina replaced Snetkova, Shiripina was supposed to replace Romanova, and Dudinskaya took Vaganova's place. Each of these had her own inherited territory, as it were, and her own students. Selection of pupils was in their hands, aided by the Art Council of the School.

Nevertheless, already at the start of the sixties, we began to run out of teachers, and as a result several of the Kirov leading dancers were offered positions on the staff. The School's new acquisitions included Inna Zubkovskaya, Igor Tchernishov, and Anatoly Nisnevitch, who at the time were still far from retirement age. All of them certainly lacked experience, and, even more important, they did not have the real teacher's talent, in Vaganova's sense of the word. Instruction at our school was mainly a matter of prestige, since the pay was ridiculously low, so that Igor Tchernishov, a dancer of outstanding training, soon quit teaching his partnering class. He was replaced by someone else, other changes followed, and gradually the whole Vaganova-built structure of the School altered. Teachers were changed rapidly and without good reason.

The same process of general deterioration struck the male classes formerly taught by such veterans as Vladimir Ponomarev, Alexander Shavrov, and Alexander Pushkin, Nureyev's and Baryshnikov's teacher. Now even Vaganova's pupils are leaving the circle, steadily replaced by inexperienced youngsters. Semenov, with whom I danced *Swan Lake,* is already close to fifty; Dudinskaya will soon be seventy. And this today is the *crème de la crème* of the School. There is no one left on stage who could inspire today's youngsters. The best dancers have died or fled abroad or gone into retirement. Only Irina Kolpakova remains as an example of past glory. Excellence has not really gone—it is still there, but out of focus. The leaders of the Kirov are distorting their values as they are trying to catch up with time. They have to learn how to absorb the evolution that has been taking place in the West without losing the traditional values in which they excel; and even give them new life and new spirit. But this will take some time.

The life of the Kirov was inextricably bound up with the life of the School, one body with two hearts. This tradition is gradually leaving my Leningrad school, which used to be the cradle of classical ballet, but it is now re-created in New York by its former student George Balanchine. His company—the New York City Ballet—is as closely connected with its school as the Kirov was once with that of Vaganova. The American Ballet Theatre does not have even the slightest shadow of this tradition—there are no ties whatsoever between the company and its school; this is why the individual styles of dancers in the company often clash—and why ABT must organize a new school in the Kirov tradition.

And what pure joy it was for us to take part for the first time in a performance on the stage of the Kirov, where we would dance the waltz from *The Sleeping Beauty* or mice in *The Nutcracker*. It was like taking a sacrament. I'll never forget the intermissions, when we would mix with the crowd of adult dancers, crowding into the buffet to nibble on pastries. And the free tickets to matinées—we were permitted to sit in the Theatre only during the day. But how often at night I would sneak in and sit spellbound in the gallery or on the stairs somewhere. I felt I was in a temple of art, because the Kirov was just that, with all its zealous priests and votaries. And every time I watched *Giselle* or *Swan Lake*, I would feel myself to be so small, such a beginner, that I would never possibly have the strength to attain such perfection.

Of course, if things had turned out differently and dancers like Nureyev, Baryshnikov, Panov, and myself had remained there, where I now see only desolation, we undoubtedly would have taken up teaching ultimately, and continuity might have been re-established, at least for a time. But it has been hopelessly interrupted, and therefore it is not regret that has involuntarily colored these pages but nostalgic bitterness. The bitterness comes not from the fact that we are not there—it's terrible to think what sort of tombstones we all would have made in that balletic cemetery—but derives from my confused, almost unconscious homesickness for my youth and the Vaganova School, tinged with the general pall that today afflicts both the Theatre and the School. One doesn't feel homesick for ruins—one cries over them. I have nothing in common today with that former impossible daydreamer who was always tripping over her own heels. And so only a feeling of bitterness remains because I am always aware—there in the northern reaches of my consciousness—that *all that* shall not be again.

I was simply an impossible student, always going around with my head in the clouds, thinking my own thoughts, and frequently, standing at the barre, not even hearing what my teacher was saying. Absent-minded and concentrated within myself, I frequently did everything backward, which drove Shiripina crazy.

Elena Vasilievna Shiripina was nurtured by Vaganova. She had been a dancer from the corps without, evidently, any special talents. But her great teaching ability was instantly sensed by Vaganova, and she inherited Vaganova's high professionalism, strictness, and unusual rigidity: Shiripina's teaching manner sometimes bordered on outright rudeness. Our respect for her was mixed with fear. Almost every day she would use her favorite pedagogical stunt on one of us, and once it happened to me. I was doing tours chaînés on the diagonal and somehow lost my sense of direction. Shiripina calmly commanded, "Keep going, little one, keep going all the way to the door." I obediently followed her instructions—and found myself outside in the hall, with the door slammed in my face!

Shiripina would even make fun of the big bosoms of some of the girls: "Do your port de bras more carefully. That's the only way to hide your boobs." Or: "To match those balloons, you're going to need a big cop with two guns." I was her special pupil, but even toward me she was excessively demanding. She constantly tried to keep me terrified—and she succeeded. If we were to raise our right arms, I would raise my left; if everyone turned in one direction, I'd insist on turning the other way. My arms simply would not listen to orders; it was as if they were living their own intensive life, and for a long while I was unable to do a proper port de bras.

Eventually I did manage to keep my arms under control and give them a certain expressiveness. Probably the happiest day in school for me was the first time Elena Vasilievna took me into a classroom, put me at the barre, and said, "Jump." I did, and she looked at the class and said, "See how she does it—and nobody taught her." It is possible that my earlier work in gymnastics helped in this: I could bend as if made of rubber, and the flips I did in the middle of the room so startled my mother that she would drop a plate.

I suffered from my absent-mindedness because it was the only stumbling block in my studies, but I could not do anything with myself. I was an escapist by nature—I still am—and had only a tangential relationship with reality. This was probably the reason for my far from simple relations with my classmates. I did not have any friends. I was meek, not aggressive, and that hidden destructiveness adolescents can display did not meet with any resistance from me. My distracted ways were taken by the other girls as a kind of proof of my muddle-headedness. In order to defend myself in some fashion, I worked hard to get top marks, to show them and myself that I wasn't stupid. I knew I wasn't, but when you live under fire you sometimes get lost yourself and forget to ask "Who am I?" Then I began to assert myself to the point of silliness. Trying to show the others that I was no downtrodden sheep, I was the first person in my class to start smoking. In the washroom during class breaks, I even taught the other girls how to inhale.

Above: At Yuri Soloviev's graduation, 1958:
BLUE BIRD *pas de deux*

Right: At fifteen: The Albéniz Serenade

Later, I was flirting with a most handsome boy in my class, and I made the claim that I could eat six quarts of ice cream (saving up for it from the money Mother gave me for lunches) and brought shame on myself—I couldn't get more than four quarts down. The taunts diminished, but I triumphed completely only much later, performing in student productions, as I gradually broke away from the ranks of my classmates and, from an ill-starred pupil, became what is called a ballerina.

Around the time I got partly free of my classmates' banter, I turned into a rather introverted girl, and the more I felt myself an outcast among them, the more I learned to value the safety of my inner haven, that small world inside me. I entered it without a backward glance, not knowing at the time that it was called "the spiritual life" or "the life of the spirit," of which I later on read so much in the books of the Russian religious philosophers, Berdyaev and others. I discovered their invaluable works only in the West, since in Russia they are accessible only to specialists.

I did not even try, in school, to analyze my feelings—I enjoyed myself in their fullness; they were impenetrable to others. This is not to say that I was entirely childish or immature, but even at sixteen or seventeen, nearing the end of school, I did not attempt to develop my reason; I simply stored up feelings, and my feelings poured out in the dance, in spite of myself, involuntarily; I didn't even try to control them. Of the school concerts, which we worked long and hard at preparing, I remember my first one in particular: I did a Spanish dance to the music of Albéniz, and danced it with gusto and absolute abandon. And when I was finished, I was surprised to hear someone behind me say: "What a little girl, and did you see the look in her eyes?" What my eyes expressed I do not know, but later I was told that there had been in my dancing much of the reserved, hidden temperament of the flamenco, and no affectation and no salivating in various directions, as with Anisimova and Gensler, who were considered specialists in the genre. I was completely overcome. After all, I had simply moved as the choreography had dictated, without having before me—at my age— any dramatic goals and without practicing any self-control.

Later, I started to learn how to control my emotions, to take some dramatic direction: "Today, I'll do thus and so to create an atmosphere for myself before going on stage." But, strangely enough, all my intentions were swept away more often than not, as if by some other will, and I would dance listening only to the voice of my body. And I could not possibly yet feel real self-control, as the essence of Vaganova's method lay in developing the spiritual element latent in every child's soul. Her method, based on the gradual conditioning of the muscles, prepared us technically for the future execution of various classical steps, but also taught us to express ourselves in dance, to fill our movements with emotional meaning.

The natural possibilities of a human body were the cornerstone of

Vaganova's system. She worked out a logical sequence of combinations that helped the body to find a way to the correct execution of prescribed movements, to develop its own coordination. The sequence of movements in class was always chosen with a logic corresponding to the natural response of the body, to the contracting abilities of the muscles. That is why Alexander Ivanovich Pushkin never gave any "corrections" to his students; instead, he tried to find the combinations that would induce their bodies to work correctly. At the same time, the class was conceived in such a way as to make all parts of the body—hands, legs, feet, toes, back, and head—combine their movements into what became a classical harmony.

Vaganova's system was based on the sense of movement: the students had to feel it physically, to realize its taste, to digest it, to make it natural for the body; the process was rational and sensual at the same time. No one tried to give the students a recipe, how one *should* sense one or another movement. In the very approach to the execution of a movement there was a certain sensual irrationality. Each student had to adapt the movement to his individual biological and psychological characteristics: each one had to master the movement guided by his own instinct. This irrationality of the initial approach seems to be the most characteristic feature of the Russian school, in contrast to the Western approach, dominated by a strict rationality dictating the mechanical execution of movements—almost like a task in gymnastics put before the body.

Vaganova's system absorbed the experience of the Russian, French, and Italian schools, and, for the first time in ballet history, she worked out scientific principles of body control, based on the study of natural body reactions. Throughout the mid-thirties, Vaganova worked on perfecting her method. None of her colleagues—not Kschessinskaya or Preobrajenskaya or Egorova—had a similar system. At that time classical ballet in Russia was not yet systematized. Those dancers who found themselves outside Russia after the Revolution were excellent professionals, but each of them had her own individual method, habits, and devices.

Many Russian dancers were brought together by Diaghilev. After his death, they dispersed all over the world and became ballet teachers, but none of them knew the Vaganova method worked out on a scientific basis and tested by many years of practice. They did not have a common style or common principles; each of them did what he was able to do. The fact that they all at one time were members of the Diaghilev company in no way guaranteed a true knowledge of the Russian dance school as it had existed for the previous forty years. To a certain extent, this school was a myth born in the West: in the 1920's it was not even formed; it was yet in the "fermentation" stage, although it brought to life a few brilliant teachers like Nikolai Legat and Olga Preobrajenskaya.

Vaganova's invaluable contribution was that, instead of separating the Russian tradition of emotional dancing (so obvious in folk dances, where every movement is born inside the dancer's body) from technical skills, she brought them together and fused them. She did not follow the Western recipe: "Learn first, and only after that express yourself"; she transformed the learning process into a continuity that from the very first steps combined mastery of the dance grammar with the emotional motivation of its primary elements.

When we came to the Vaganova School, we were unaware of the spirit that lived in every one of us. But children are naturally emotional—their inner life follows laws often alien and incomprehensible to adults. Some children are as pliable as wax and can be shaped into almost anything. The important goal was to help them develop a sense of movement, not by merely giving them a technical recipe but by using technical exercises as a means to reveal their inner emotional potential, to make them aware of it, to enable them to use it in class.

From the first lesson we were warned against a formal execution of a movement, even if it was a mere battement tendu. Formalism is alien to Russian culture in general, not only to the Russian school of ballet. The ability to sense a movement, no matter how simple, and to fill it with spiritual meaning was developed step by step, by hard everyday training. Of course, to develop such abilities, the student must possess them in the first place, even if only in embryo. This ability, whenever it is there, cannot be overlooked, and today I can immediately spot those in the beginners' class who have it and those who do not, the ones who need developing and perfecting of it and the ones who need first to be made aware of it. This ability displays itself in the simplest of gestures, in the way one opens the arms, points the toes, or controls the chest. Essentially, it is a capacity of the body to generate a specific kind of energy in movement that affects an observer in class and, later, a spectator in the theatre. Of course, these shapes and lines of the body are given to us at birth—for instance, my arms and hands, which lead some people to speak about the "romantic nature" of my body and my "plastique végétale," were completely formed by the time I was seventeen, in my fourth year of school. Such physical qualities of a body are inborn, and very often they determine the character of the roles the dancer will be able to perform—romantic, classical, or neoclassical. Line, however, is not an end in itself. One must learn to make one's body line sing in dance, and irradiate the specific energy that can be generated only if one's inner sensations transform themselves into a visual expression.

When many years later I staged "The Kingdom of the Shades" scene from *La Bayadère* for American Ballet Theatre, I had to explain to the corps de ballet something that was as clear to me as the multiplication table because it had been drummed into me at school. As my teacher Shiripina had made me understand then, I now explained to them (my English

still very rough) that it is, for instance, not permissible to perform an arabesque in a formal manner—instead it should exude flight, lightness, pur-
posefulness. This was a revelation to them. They did not understand that
the difference between "executing steps" and "dancing steps" is approximately the same as the difference between "Gracious Sir" and "Your
Grace." They had been taught to move, and many of them were very good
at it, doing fouettés and tours I might have envied. But the coloration, the
emotional tonality in movement that gave the ballet its infectious poetry,
was absent for them. And it's amazing that as soon as they mastered this
coloration, they were set free. They danced the celebrated "Shades" no less
well than the corps de ballet at the Kirov.

My services in this were minimal; everything should be attributed to the
Vaganova method, which has not infrequently shown its capacity to live in
Western soil.

"To execute a step" and "to dance a step"—the opposition of these two
concepts contains within itself the entire history of the classical dance.
People often say that the classical ballet is devoid of emotion, that it's simply a beautiful geometric regulation of movement set to music and pleasing
to the eye. And it's said that the libretti of most of the older ballets are
completely nonsensical—all those "maidens of the Danube," a collection of
melodramatic episodes dragged out into four acts; the plot is simply not important, as in the traditional Italian opera, which merely requires beauty of
vocal performance, while the ballet demands above all a technical virtuosity
not always to be identified with artistry.

The opinion that the classical ballet is essentially a set of formal stunts
is totally alien to me, though the great theorist Noverre himself expressed
it. I have read that the classical dance is conventional and that the dancer's
body does not so much define the structure of the pas as serve as one of its
most beautiful conventions. All my balletic experience protests against
these determinations.

Of course, classical ballet has its own grammar—all those arabesques!
—and it is a formal grammar, as the iambs and trochees of poetry are formal. But this is purely theoretical. Movement does not exist outside the human body, and if a dancer's body is incapable of filling movement with
meaning, in order to convey to the audience an equivalent mood, a sense
of life, in order to *disturb,* then such a body has no place in the ballet. For
me, dancing means overcoming that formality of movement, it means spirituality—otherwise what good is it?

The concept of "spirituality" in the Russian ballet was born with the appearance of Anna Pavlova, the incarnation of the eternal feminine, of "the
dancing of the soul," on stage. If you look through reviews of ballets in old
Russian newspapers, you will be amused by the picture that emerges. In

the beginning, the critics—and they were the best of the audience—
approached the ballet from a strictly formal point of view: "Miss Andrianova
executed grandes cabrioles en avant well." Or: "Instead of fouettés, Egorova
danced *la crème fouettée*." In Russia, Andrei Levinson and Akim Volynsky
were the first, inspired by Pavlova, to equate genius—not formal beauty—
with spiritual dance. For me, a ballerina who does not have emotional impact is not a ballerina; she is merely a dancer, an artisan, even if her technique is fantastic. Ballerinas of formal virtuosity who spin like a top seem
to me much more boring than a spiritualized but technically less-brilliant
ballerina. Technical flaws can be corrected, but there is nothing to be done
with a body capable only of what, in olden times, was called *des morceaux
de virtuosité*. Luckily, no one yet gives formal classes in inspiration!

I have frequently asked myself why people go to the same classical ballets again and again. I do not mean the balletomaniacs but simple mortals
who may have seen *Swan Lake* a dozen times. Not for the suspense of the
story, long familiar, do these witnesses to space flights and heart trans-
plants go to the theatre. And what, to them, is the suffering of a girl in the
shape of a swan, taken from an old fairy tale? Are they bewitched by the
technical stunts of the dancers—let's say the ill-fated thirty-two fouettés,
the execution of which they follow intently and with the same ardor as if
they were at the circus? But the classical ballet is not a circus; it lacks that
sharpness and variety of surprises with which the circus arena is so rich,
those miracles of muscular energy and of skill. Then maybe it is the beauty
of the geometric constructions of a Petipa or an Ivanov? Yet these are re-
petitive and, like anything formal, can easily pall. Or is the ballet capable
of emanating a particular emotional charge, a current of spirituality that
goes straight to the spectator's heart?

I feel that this is everything. Classical ballet is, in this sense, closer to
music than anything else. In music, sound is arranged harmoniously, and
what it asserts can be only partially rendered in words. In the classical
ballet, it is the body, subject to the harmony of the steps it is executing,
which speaks. And it speaks to the heart in as direct a language as does
music. Of course, the body's range of meaning is more limited—it cannot
completely overcome its concreteness—and it can only make music concrete, translating its abstract language into plastic form. I believe that the
body can overcome its corporeality through the magic of inspiration and can
be transfigured into a musical phrase. But how to accomplish this? It cannot be taught, and however much I have tried to find the magical formula,
I have been unable to. It is possible that I am encroaching now on the very
secret of art and of inspiration, and it has not been given to anyone to deci-
pher it.

We were not given classes in inspiration at the Vaganova School, but we
were taught how to express ourselves through the formal grammar of the
classical dance, through that same arabesque. Indeed, emotional coloration

depends entirely on the inner state of your heroine, on the dramatic collision which casts its light upon you. And thousands of meanings are born. Take, for instance, Odette's arabesques in the second act; they are passionate, bursting with the desire to break free, with grief, with consciousness of impending doom, anything you like. And if these subtleties are not rendered, then without knowing the libretto, it will be quite impossible to follow what is happening. Odile's arabesques are enticing, intimating trial and ruination. But there is another possible reading of this step. Giselle's arabesque is incorporeal, airy, the arabesque of a phantom that is the very substance of the feminine.

The same variety of meanings is to be read in the saut de basque, in all forms of the jeté; meaning and poetry derive from overcoming their formality. Take even the pas de chat; the very term assumes sinuous, cat-like movements, airiness, lightness. Generally speaking, this is one of the ways of cutting through scenic space and rendering it diverse. But it may be performed forcefully or with extreme sharpness, or the dancer may soar weightlessly—everything is dictated by the inner state and dramatic necessity. Whereas turned-in positions are closed, introverted, and are by nature full of meaning, and it was natural for Fokine to see in them an expression of blustery, stormy psychology. Thus, if the classical dance has a grammar, it is in fact a spiritualized grammar. Otherwise, there would not be various interpretations, various Odettes, Giselles, Auroras.

Of course, great dancers are born with this feeling for the spiritual, as lyric poets are born, as Ulanova had it. She was able to take even the most inexpressive, trite movements, for instance as Maria in *The Fountain of Bakhchisarai,* to the realm of pure poetry.

I have spoken so insistently and so frequently of this spirituality in my interviews in the West that I was once asked: "But what is a ballerina to do if she has only technique, if she's as empty as a mannequin inside?" Once again, I answer: "Either develop the habits of the inner life or do not go into the classical ballet, for it is not a circus."

The body never lies, and the dance, and every ballet lesson as well, is like a confession. Each time I approach the barre, I begin an unequal duel with my own body, which rebels like an untrained horse. There is a special pleasure and a special satisfaction in this, an almost masochistic pleasure in the body's rebelling, its aching and hurting. And you bring it under control and make it responsive to that which the soul is eager to make manifest. And you become a ballerina for your entire life, for to become a ballerina means to bring into ideal balance the essentially instrumental, physical possibilities of your capricious, imperfect body with the possibilities of your soul, which is eternally renewing itself and constantly demanding new expression.

Having finished school, I was far from possessing this happy balance.

Theoretically, the Vaganova system, which provides for a natural and gradual transition from simple movements to more complex ones, is appropriate for anyone who has the necessary physical ability for the dance. I did, but, because of my wild scurrying about in school, I did not succeed in mastering the technique properly. There simply was not sufficient time. What is more, as I have said, I had naturally rather soft legs, so I learned to perform fouettés only when I was entrusted with my first *Swan* at the Kirov. I began with four fouettés and gradually increased the number toward the required thirty-two!

At this time when I would fall about from two relevés, I struggled everywhere with my technical flaws: at the barre, in rehearsals, and preparing for school concerts, which I approached with extraordinary seriousness. I danced one of the four gypsies from *La Esmeralda,* which gave me my first stimulating experience of the "sense of ensemble"; a waltz to someone's music, I've forgotten whose, and the white adagio from *Swan Lake.* (The waltz was presented by the young Oleg Vinogradov, who now vainly clutches the choreographic reins of the Kirov in his hands, working against a host of inconceivable restraints.)

I was supposed to perform the *Swan Lake* adagio in my final examination, but again I was lucky. By pure chance, I was given the adagio from the second act of *Giselle.* At first it had been given to my schoolmate Liuda Kovaleva, but her teacher, Komkova, decided that she could show off her solid technique better in the *Swan Lake* pas de deux, while I, whose virtuosity left a good deal to be desired, got *Giselle.*

My partner was Nikita Dolgushin, long-legged, sensitive, with a slightly elongated, Mediterranean face, and black, flashing eyes. Nikita was born a romantic dancer; in his restrained manner there was a delightful elegance. He was refined and intellectual, which was a great help to me in my first work on *Giselle.* He explained many things to me, and between us there arose that emotional field of mutual understanding, mutual attraction, which I value so much in a partner. And even on the surface, everyone said, we made an extremely expressive pair. I worked on the adagio less than I should have, since doing it had come like a bolt from the blue. And I worked on it intuitively of course, relying on my feelings, to which, with naïve irresponsibility, I gave free rein. Our success surpassed all expectations. The critics took note of us—the extremely observant Vera Krasovskaya saw in our diligent, though undoubtedly timorous, performance a contemporary interpretation: intellectually chilling, overshadowing the elegiac sorrow of the duet; even a drama of misunderstanding.

Arriving at school in the morning, I was struck by my triumph. It was my first taste of notoriety, flattering to any actor; moreover, I was even recognized on the street, to the great astonishment of my mother, who could not at first get used to my success. A reputation as a romantic ballerina was established for me—my long neck, long legs, light and brittle line, and the very contour of my body recalled, people said, the lithographs of Grisi and Taglioni.

Encouraged by this talk, I tried at first to emphasize the plastic resemblance with posing—by a turn of the head, by a movement of the hands. I liked these stylistic contrivances—and in fact, the duet from *Giselle* was not my first attempt at romanticism. A year before the final examination I danced *The Poet and His Muse* to the music of Liszt, staged most inventively by Kasian Goleizovsky, whose choreography—romantic plasticity which had fortunately absorbed sharp, angular elements of neoclassicism—was close to my soul. I danced it with Dolgushin, who came out on stage in a blond wig which created a lively impression of Liszt's long, stringy hair; he groped in the air with his fingers, as it were, for the first chord of the famous "Dreams of Love." Representing his Muse, I was in a romantic white tunic, behind him, doing an arabesque, as if directing and inflaming his imagination. The partnership beteen Nikita and me sprang up immediately. How painful it is that he was not given a chance, and that we, an ideal romantic pair, danced together so little.

After my final examination, I was taken into the Kirov company. I was not happy about that at all. I did not want too easy a career; like many Russians who read too much Dostoevsky, I was fascinated by the idea of suffering, and I thought that in the Siberian wilds it would be much more difficult for me and, therefore, more exciting. What's more, I was deathly afraid of the Kirov when I showed up there in the autumn of 1959.

DANCING IN RUSSIA

In memoriam: Yuri Soloviev

Crossing the threshold of the Kirov Theatre as a member of the corps de ballet, I felt nothing except overwhelming, paralyzing fear. Everyone looked so important and unapproachable; I didn't know what to do with myself from shyness, and blushed red at every glance thrown my way by the men.

The atmosphere in the Theatre was much like that in the School: the same solemnity entreating us to Serve Art. When I went into a classroom or rehearsal hall, my knees would be shaking and I would feel sick in the pit of my stomach. Fortunately, I was not in the corps long; my forgetfulness and distracted wandering about continued to assert themselves there. But at least I didn't join the "strict ranks" of the corps de ballet, where my slip-ups were an affront to its uniform beauty. Many at the Kirov still remember how impossible I was with all my hilarious mistakes.

It was not simply a matter of being unable to concentrate and get my bearings. What in Russia is called "the feeling for the collective" was, on the whole, absent in me. I do not love crowds—I fear them—and any sort of mob or collective mentality distresses me. I am incapable of merging with the human mass, because I immediately experience, almost as a reflex, the desire to shut myself off and to retreat into myself. It's possible that this is my natural self-defense, that somewhere in the depths of my subconscious there's a childish fear that was reinforced by the excessive aggressiveness of my schoolmates.

In any case, I danced a swan in *Swan Lake* and one of the shadows in the last act of *La Bayadère*, and was noticed by Fenster, who was artistic director of the Kirov at the time. (Konstantin Sergeyev, who was alternately appointed to and removed from this post, became firmly entrenched in it a little later.) Fenster said of me, "She's a good girl, only a trifle heavy. She's got to lose some weight."

A certain roundness and softness of line did not bother me very much in a romantic tunic, though. In fact, after the success of the pas de deux from *Giselle* in my final exam, that ballet immediately became identified with me. At first, I danced a sylphide in *Les Sylphides*, then, on December 27, 1959, I performed my first complete *Giselle*, with Nikita Dolgushin as Albrecht. That evening began what was for me an intense and dramatic relationship with this ballet, which I have now danced innumerable times. No other ballet was so compatible with my physical characteristics, nor brought me such success and creative satisfaction, and I have thought about and sweated over no other ballet so much as *Giselle*. Therefore, I cannot help returning to it again and again. At that time, because of my youth and inexperience, I did not set any dramatic objectives for myself. I was nineteen; Giselle, apparently, seventeen, and the medieval legend excited me more than the stage setting. I simply put on a dress with bodice and apron and—keeping in mind that my Giselle had just awakened from a refreshing sleep, bright and ready to meet the stranger who had fallen in love with her—left her village cottage and went on stage.

Learning something by rote was never a problem with me; everything was already "in the feet," as they say, and I set out with enthusiasm and diligence to dance Giselle. For the first time, I experienced the joy of merging my self with my village girl, a merging that was completely spontaneous and unrehearsed. I did not try, as debutantes frequently do, to imitate anyone—not even Liane Daydé, whom I had seen during the Paris Opera's tour of Russia in 1958. She had impressed me with the meticulousness of her stylistic touches and, in the second act, the flawlessness of position which called to mind the romantic lithographs of Carlotta Grisi.

I was myself, and my Giselle turned out to be peculiar (not to say iconoclastic), as far as tradition goes. I was too lively, coquettish, made eyes at Albrecht, shrugged my shoulders, plucked mincingly at my apron. Vera Krasovskaya, a superb critic of the ballet with whom I have discussed the details as well as the basic problem of Giselle more than once (should I forgive Albrecht or not, and so on), not without reason saw in my first major role "a young girl from the big city, trembling under a protective covering of independence," rather than a romantic heroine over whom hangs a sad fate. In other words, I was completely out of character in the first act. I overdid the mad scene and then died much too theatrically. I did not know any limitations or balance—that distance between me, Natasha Makarova, and Giselle, without which it is impossible to achieve either faithfulness to the romantic style or its contemporary resonance.

Yet my romantic qualities were particularly appropriate to the Kirov's traditions, since the romantic style was an inherent property of the theatre, going back to the old Maryinsky. By "romantic style" I mean something broad—not only *Giselle, La Sylphide,* or *Les Sylphides,* but, in part, *Swan Lake* too, where the refined purity of romantic composition was so skillfully made weightier by Lev Ivanov, in the second act, with the symbolic dimension he added to the general style.

I associate the romantic style with absolute harmony of all elements: delicate sketching of the plastic representation, airiness and lightness in transmission of emotions which cannot be captured in words. And this style, cherished for almost a century and a half, was so much a part of the Kirov Theatre of the late fifties and early sixties! The pure aristocratic quality of pose and port de bras, the purity of classic positions, all the geometry of beauty and the beauty of geometry which was sown in Russian soil by Marius Petipa. It reverberated with the architectonics of the city itself, where French classicism and a certain spirit of the Italian baroque merged so harmoniously. The Kirov style is determined by strict traditions of a culture which always stood behind St. Petersburg; it was there, in fact, that in the beginning of this century, in a truly European way, the poetry of the Symbolists and the Acmeists blossomed. Blok, Akhmatova, and Mandelstam were in Petersburg, not in Moscow, where Mayakovsky, Pasternak, and

Tsvetaeva, with Muscovite daring and unmindful of tradition, rebelled.

Moscow does not have Petersburg's European traditions, just as it lacks unity. It was and is a Tartar city, a mixture of styles, sprawling, colorful, somewhat mercantile. All this is reflected in the Bolshoi's style, which would seem to have developed at the expense of the Kirov. The Bolshoi's best dancers and teachers were stolen from us: Elizaveta Pavlovna Gerdt, who shaped Plisetskaya and Maximova; Ulanova, Semyonova, Yermolaev, Koren and Nina Timofeyeva, and Yury Grigorovich, who came later. The Bolshoi did not create its own style, but rather a patchwork like Moscow it-self. Its dancers took advantage of this. Not bound by tradition and a sense of continuity, they could break with the old more easily, throwing the doors wide open to experimentation and innovation, although this sometimes came off clumsily.

The Kirov guarded its past far too jealously, maintaining it like an old garden, and, busy with its own honest labor, did not notice (and did not want to notice) that it is also necessary to know how to cultivate a new garden.

The Bolshoi was in no danger of turning into a museum; it was dynamic in its lack of a style, and not without allure. Against this background, Ulanova looked like a rare Petersburg bird. Plisetskaya, on the other hand, with her ostentatious disregard of tradition and her bacchic temperament, is a phenomenon particularly characteristic of Moscow. In Leningrad, willful-ness like hers might have been—and was—condemned. But then there is the Bolshoi's production of *Les Sylphides,* which I was not able to sit through. It simply lacked the Petersburg aesthetic and looked almost like a parody.

From the first at the Kirov I was loaded down with almost the entire repertoire: other classics besides *Giselle, Les Sylphides,* and *Swan Lake;* old Soviet ballets which had already been pronounced golden treasures of national choreography—*The Fountain of Bakhchisarai* by Zakharov, Lavrovsky's *Romeo and Juliet;* and new things as well, such as Fenster's *Masquerade,* after Lermontov's drama.

Nina in *Masquerade* and Maria in *The Fountain* gave me very little ar-tistic challenge, though these ballets were supposed to be distinguished by the dramatic (or to be truthful, the melodramatic). Nina, a sort of Russian variation of Desdemona, is dying from poison provided by her jealous hus-band, Arbenin. Maria, a Polish princess who finds herself in the harem of Girei, a Tarter khan who loves her, is killed by the dagger of the insanely jealous first wife of the harem, Zarema. But the choreography of these pieces is primitive, static, more often than not merely illustrative of the melodramatic twists of plot. I simply died of boredom and did not know how to make these heroines interesting to myself, if no one else.

GISELLE, *1961*

Maria is one of Ulanova's famous roles. I saw her Maria on film and marveled at how she was able to raise such a choreographic primitive to the level of poetry. Struck in the back by Zarema's dagger, Maria—Ulanova —slipped slowly down next to a smooth column, collapsing almost with acceptance, like a plant, a flower. . . . I was not doing anything like this, and was not able to. Any kind of acceptance and peace was incompatible with me. Bursting with feeling, I was buffeted in many directions; anything passive or sacrificial was alien.

I rehearsed Juliet, from Lavrovsky's ballet, with Tatiana Mikhailovna Vecheslova. In the past, she had been Vakhtang Chabukiani's partner, and they both danced extensively in the West during the thirties, presenting the new Soviet ballet. Tatiana was primarily a dramatic ballerina, an actress, who never distinguished herself technically but whose artistry was in her blood. Esmeralda, from Pugni's ballet of the same name; Zarema; Tao-hoa, from *The Red Poppy*—this was her element. Tatiana left the stage at the height of her career, having decided not to becloud the audience's memory of her triumphs by final performances (at which the public usually experiences respect tinged with nostalgia rather than real ecstasy).

Tempestuous, passionate, with a sharp tongue, Tatiana was a remarkable showman. I, too, was extremely impetuous. I, too, did not know restraint, and the two of us together in a rehearsal hall were really too much. At rehearsals, a sort of agitated, electric atmosphere prevailed: I was fired by Tatiana's artistry and did everything full force. She gave approval excitedly, but to our mutual horror everything that we would work out one day would disappear the next. I worked on Juliet with Tatiana in this way for a month, which was rather a long time. Formerly, roles were rehearsed as much as half a year, but this tradition had come to an end by my day: I danced *Raymonda* after only two rehearsals.

My rehearsals with Tatiana were more like improvisations on assigned themes. It was my fault—at the time, I was organically incapable of remembering a device, a detail, or a dramatic coloration, whether it was something I myself had come upon or something suggested by Tatiana. Each time I did everything differently, and Tatiana started to lose patience. Rehearsals turned into a sort of mini-performance; there was no way to curb my spontaneity.

But that was not the only thing. I did not have any emotional contact with Lavrovsky's choreography. In the thirties he had created *Romeo and Juliet* with Ulanova in mind, her stasis, her gesture and animated expressiveness of pose. But I am not by nature a static ballerina. I need some kind of dance movement. Moreover, a sort of sixth sense told me—I understood this only much later—that there was a split between Prokofiev's music with its disharmonious harmony, its nervous, impulsive nature, and Lavrovsky's old-fashioned, illustrative transcription. There was nothing contemporary in it for me. My body responded to the music instantaneously, then it would get stuck like a bird in a snare in the worn combinations of endless arabesques and glissades, in the pantomime which was stifling the ballet. In everything I felt a certain *démodé* quality, an unnaturalness. The choreography did not even seem comic to me, but decrepit, almost silly.

I remember how I carried on before Friar Laurence gave me the poison. Why was it necessary for me to run to the door behind which my parents, angry at my disobedience, were hidden, then run back again? I felt no naturalness in this; the balletic convention itself looked forced. And I suffered, trying to squeeze myself into this dilapidated style and at the same time appear contemporary. But the reaction of my body to Prokofiev's music did not correspond to the constrained plastique; I was involuntarily trying to express the music *in spite of* the style. This was perceived by Vera Krasovskaya, who had come to watch our noisy rehearsals and later wrote precisely and realistically of the performance: "Makarova needs a new design, a whole new cloth more likely. She would need a new dance vocabulary too, sharper, more piercing, more dance-like, which would render the hopelessness of Juliet's lonely rebellion. . . . Daring, quarrelsome, nimble, she could protest more firmly, throw down challenges more boldly to the 'establishment,' if terseness in responding and monotony of plastic expression had not limited her so. Dance which expresses all the complexity of musical imagery—not gestures illustrating the text of a play—such is the demand of the times, which means the internal demand of the actress, whose art is a contemporary one."

Now Lavrovsky's old-fashionedness is more than obvious to me, and I was truly shocked when, two years ago in London, Svetlana Beriosova told me that she wanted to dance his Juliet because it seemed to her that there was something genuinely dramatic about the part. But for me, no matter how many times I have seen this Juliet (with the exception of Ulanova, who transformed it into a miracle), the performance either has been boring in its slavish adherence to the choreography or simply underlined the gulf between the dance vocabulary and the score.

With every performance of *Romeo and Juliet,* I would think up something new, and sometimes, taking the fatal potion and lying down on the bed as the curtain came down, I would think that now, today, I had gotten everything out of it that I ever could. But my friends would tell me quite frankly that nothing had happened. Other times, having danced in complete control, which was so difficult for me to do then, I would hear cries of: "Now today it was all right!" I still do not know why. Of course, the audience's perception of a role and the actor's rarely correspond, but with my Juliet they never corresponded at all. And no matter how many times Tatiana would patiently set the gesture for me or polish the positioning of my Juliet, the role never brought me any satisfaction.

GISELI

left: BLUE BIRD *pas de deux*

right: The Kirov Theatre

tom left: LES SYLPHIDES, *with Sergei Vikulov*

tom right: GISELLE

I worked with Vecheslova on *Swan Lake,* too. It was true torture. No other role came with more difficulty for me, none was so exhausting. First of all, Ivanov-Petipa's choreography doesn't tolerate any spontaneity, to which I am very much inclined. Each movement is to be executed one way and one way only. You are obliged to adhere strictly to the academic grammar. In Act II, I was able to follow those mechanical rules, but that was not the problem. It was Odile's choreography in Act III that became a real ordeal; the density of her choreographic texture was simply too much for me. My stamina was not great enough to cope with the high speed of her turns or renversés. As a romantic ballerina, I never needed to be good at pirouettes and the like; my artistic strength lay in the flow of my movement. Even the best thing I had at the time—my arms—even they lived, so to speak, their own individual, intense life. All the same, Tatiana set them for me and forced me to beat them. And what was most amazing was that the sensation of wings was strengthened. Dudinskaya, with whom I rehearsed *Swan Lake* somewhat later, was quite unable to give me this feeling; she never had possessed wings herself. But Tatiana did. And the two teachers complemented each other wonderfully. Dudinskaya worked on my endurance, my stamina; Tatiana taught me to be an actress.

And so my lyricism could somehow pull me through as Odette, even if my feet slipped out from under me. But at the thought of Odile I would simply grow cold from terror. I hate my early photographs as Odile—a coquettish flirt, nice-looking, with chiselled (and, alas, excessively soft) legs; charming, but not evil. I dashed into the Queen's ball, turned the Prince's head, twirled and spun around (and not much of that, to speak frankly), and disappeared. Almost a grisette. There was not a hint of the aggressive, triumphant attitude of the *femme fatale.* And how I feared my pirouettes and fouettés! I hunched my shoulders in fear, and, to be honest, I did not give a single first-rate performance of *Swan Lake* in Russia. Only in the West was I freed of my "swan complex."

Both my very first and my very last performances of *Swan Lake* in Leningrad resulted in embarrassments, of which I luckily recall only a few. The stumbling block (always a most appropriate term) was Odile's final thirty-two fouettés, symbolizing the complete triumph of the envoy of evil. At my first performance, I finished the fouettés in a rear wing; after the first ten bars no one on stage could see me anymore. It was as if I had been blown off-stage by the wind. Anyway, I might have fallen flat (as Maya Plisetskaya once did, after which she substituted tours piqués for the ill-fated fouettés), or been carried toward the footlights (as happened once long ago to Marina Semyonova, who on the twentieth turn almost ended up in the orchestra pit). Ballerinas are usually drawn toward the footlights. But, no, everything was the other way around with me; for some reason I was drawn backward into the wings. At my last *Swan* before leaving for London in

1970, after a series of brilliant rehearsals at which everything went beautifully, an absolute catastrophe occurred. Dancing Odile's variation in the
black pas de deux, I slipped from a pirouette in attitude and froze on the
spot from shock. I felt completely empty, didn't understand anything that I
was doing, and began the variation again, only to fail again. Then I dashed
into the wings. The conductor and the musicians stopped, terrified. I was
hysterical. Someone cried: "Get back on stage and try again." I was literally shoved back on the stage, and I finished the pas de deux to the encouraging applause of the audience.

In order to dance *Swan Lake* well (in the sense of internal satisfaction),
in those years I needed a lot of intellectual encouragement. A phrase which
sounded like a subtle formula, an intelligent conversation which awakened
my thoughts, was capable of stirring me more than dozens of rehearsals. So
it was; so it remains today. Life's vicissitudes do not have as much power
over my imagination as music, art, or what is called intellectual conversation. I recall that one of my most successful *Swan*s was a matinée, after an
absolutely insane night in the house of Igor Tchernishov. We talked almost
until morning, and I went on stage with very little sleep. Night talk in
Russia is a very old tradition. At table with tea or a bottle of wine, the
conversation goes on far beyond midnight, confidential, secret, covering
anything you please: problems of art, personal confusions, and so on.

The talk with Igor about *Swan Lake* came up spontaneously and therefore acted as a profound stimulus to me. I started to complain that I was
fed up with dancing *Swan Lake* in a single emotional key, that I had to
think up fresh accents. (Just when I had succeeded in getting "fed up" with
Swan Lake is not clear.) Igor gave rein to his very rich fantasy. The details
of the conversation have faded from memory, of course, but he was propos-
ing something absolutely unusual and quite unacceptable to me. I started
arguing . . . I rehearsed practically the entire performance in their tiny
kitchen, while Igor and his wife, Elena, encouraged me: "Now, here, instead of that . . . do a deep plié and change the lines of the hands." And
so on in that vein. And as a result the image of the performance, my
Odette and Odile, somehow changed internally for me; it is difficult even to
say how. And I danced the matinée with a great emotional uplift. Even
Sergeyev said to me after the performance: "Oh, Natashka, how inventive
you are. A real decadent." What it was that was decadent I do not now recall, and I was unable to keep hold of the accents, unfortunately. The performance was pure improvisation, and like everything impromptu it disappeared just as spontaneously as it had appeared. At that time, had I the
control which I have now acquired, had I been able to fix emotions in my
mind and turn them into dramatic devices, it is possible that I would have
approached sooner that much better *Swan Lake* which I danced many years
later in the West.

If Vecheslova fostered my artistry, then Natalia Mikhailovna Dudinskaya developed my stamina, which was sorely lacking in those days. Occasionally, my partially trained body did not withstand the frenzied schedule with which I was saddled at the Kirov. In addition to everything else, I continued to be as absent-minded on stage as before, which, together with weak technique, can lead to some confusing results. And it did . . .

In *Don Quixote*, dancing one of the flower girls—Juanita or something like that—I almost collapsed from the excessive tension of the coda. I started to retch right on stage and dashed for the wings and the bathroom. My partner, Sakhnovskaya, to her great surprise, remained alone to dance the coda for both of us and all but froze from astonishment when I, now feeling better, came straight back on stage to take a bow. I could not miss that, since Sergeyev would never forgive one's taking such a liberty. Another time, while performing this coda, I, like an experienced circus acrobat, ended in a split on the floor instead of the expected grand jeté. But the worst confusion occurred during a performance of *The Bronze Horseman*, while I was dancing the tiny part of the Queen of the Ball. I didn't take into consideration the weight of my petticoats, and while doing tours piqués *en dedans* I managed to fall into the prompter's box, to which my heavy attire had pulled me. I stayed there, hiding in terror like a mouse, hoping that no one would notice my mysterious disappearance. My partner couldn't think of anything better to do than start gallantly pulling me and all my skirts out of there, which he managed successfully. There was nothing to do but pretend that my dive into the box had been part of the staging.

And what terrible suffering was Pugni's *The Humpbacked Horse* and my Czar-maiden for me. She was a Czar-ballerina to whom any of the embellishments of the classical dance on Russian, French, Polish, or any other themes were nothing. Quite stupefied from the difficult stunts with which the academic *morceaux* of this part abound, I became hysterical just before the last variation and started shouting, "I won't go back on stage for anything. You want me dead!" And I grabbed onto a handrail like a bulldog. Dudinskaya and Seva Ukhov had all they could do to pull me away, then literally shove me back on stage. How I managed to finish I don't know. God helped me. In spite of all such tragedies, *The Humpbacked Horse* was a turning point; I was physically strengthened by doing it, and life became much easier.

In the past, Dudinskaya had been a phenomenal virtuoso; she was one of the best teachers at the Vaganova School and knew all my sins. She loved to recall how she first saw me and Alla Sizova (we had just graduated) as friends of the Prince in *Swan Lake*! "I had been asked to take a look at the new girls in the pas de trois. Yurochka Soloviev flitted between them, and they were up to something . . . well, what burdens God lays on

top and bottom: THE LITTLE HUMPBACKED HORSE

t top and bottom: BLUE BIRD *pas de deux, with Sergei Vikulov*

the soul." Dudinskaya was good to me and unusually strict. She was frequently accused of stifling the individuality of young ballerinas and making them copies (more often pale copies) of herself. Strangely enough, with me nothing of the kind happened. She did not interfere with my interpretations, never cut off my unrestrained flights of fancy, but concentrated only on my technique, driving and urging me on unmercifully in the classroom. She possessed such will and such uncontradictable authority that I did not dare, for instance, to break off a variation being rehearsed, however exhausted and tense I might be. I did not dare not to finish something. "Don't stop, keep going," she would demand like a sergeant major. And, afraid to indulge myself, I went on, regardless of the black circles under my eyes and my legs giving way beneath me. Her military dictates were a salvation for me then: I usually danced only three or four performances a month. With such a minimal work load I could not afford slipshod rehearsals—otherwise I simply would have fallen apart and no one would have been able to glue me back together again. In the West, where I sometimes dance fifteen or twenty performances a month, form is strengthened on stage, and I do not have to strain so at rehearsals.

Dudinskaya could be quite severe. I recall how I fell down at a rehearsal of *Cinderella* and so knocked the wind out of myself that I could not even cry out—I had dislocated my shoulder. This was just a few days before the performance. There was a commotion in the theatre; they took me to the first-aid room. Our masseuse, Antonina Ivanovna, a sort of grenadier in a skirt with huge steel hands, undertook enthusiastically (as usual) to fix my shoulder, to my wild cries. Dudinskaya came in and said quietly: "Don't worry, everything will be all right. You'll be on stage in three or four days. We, too, frequently danced in pain and hurt. It's nothing. As you see, we made it." This seemed monstrously callous to me at the time; now I understand that Dudinskaya was essentially right.

Dancers cannot be self-pitying—they must have a masochism of the ballet in their blood or they will never realize their potential. The balletic body is terribly vulnerable: merely hurt your finger, hit a corn, or rip a toenail and you are out of the ranks. We cannot be led about by our bodies or they will take over, and we are lost. In order to take the body in hand and to overcome it, we often dance "bloodied," with raw feet or terrible colds, as I have done many times. To triumph over the body, to cultivate this balletic masochism—this Dudinskaya taught me.

The artistic policy in the Kirov was formed under the strong dictatorship of Konstantin Sergeyev. At the beginning of the sixties it became a sort of patrimonial estate, and he ruled over it as a great landowner. The stunning danseur noble of the past, the partner of Ulanova, by then was finished as a classical dancer—he was almost fifty. But I managed to dance his last *Giselle* with him, and I must say that he was a brilliant partner of the old school, which made itself felt in his special manner of support. It was not simply comfortable. He was able to partner a ballerina without giving the impression of supporting her. He could sense the point of her balance and still maintain his distance. And he never exerted unnecessary strength when directing me literally with one hand, so that I never felt myself bound to my partner; I felt simultaneously free and yet in his control. Many partners expend great physical effort, but that does not necessarily lead to the most successful result. Some of my partners in the West have not been able to understand this principle at first when I explain it to them, but later they have been surprised at the apparent ease of what had seemed so difficult. The point is that partnering does not require great physical effort, but coordination in response to which the ballerina feels free in her partner's hands and which in no way restricts her own movements. I do not need to be grasped—I need to be directed, as Sergeyev did with me. Among my partners Ivan Nagy has been an exemplar of this kind of partnering, as have Erik Bruhn, Donald MacLeary, and Anthony Dowell.

From the time Sergeyev became the main choreographer at the Kirov, he tried to protect the stronghold of the classical dance from any modernistic or simply contemporary trends, and this policy was both stimulating and disastrous. Sergeyev was extremely professional, flesh and bone of the Petersburg balletic culture. He was adept at refashioning the old ballets by cutting out decrepit pantomime or outdated passages and by maintaining that culture of gesture for which the Maryinsky was famous. He could rehearse the entrance of the court ladies in the Prologue of *The Sleeping Beauty* for hours, polishing each detail. And so it went, month after month, year in, year out. Usually, a new production took a year to stage, which seems absolutely incredible by Western standards. And as a result, the level of the classics remained impeccably high and their style never lost any of its gloss or elegance.

Ambitious, intelligent, and shrewd, Sergeyev was far from being "an ordinary guy." He combined a high degree of professionalism and knowledge of the classical dance with reactionary attitudes and a rigid aesthetic presentation. Because he had got stuck in the aesthetics of the thirties and forties, he was rather militant against accepting anything newer than the standard classics. And his traditional tastes, even though reinforced with his marvelous professionalism, very often turned out badly. Sergeyev was an excellent purveyor of old masterpieces, who sincerely believed in the old tradition, worshipped Petipa and Ivanov, and was deeply concerned with preserving their genuine style, but as a choreographer he didn't impress me. This very artistic failure, however, as paradoxical as it may seem, gave him a strong position in the eyes of the Party bosses who oversaw the Kirov.

The Kirov needed Sergeyev and the authorities were pleased with him because his conservative tastes coincided with theirs. Afraid of intruders in their bureaucratic calm, they could sleep peacefully at night, secure with Sergeyev, because he could never create anything audacious, anything threatening to explode the doctrine of Socialist Realism, thereby endangering the big shots responsible for the "ideological façade of the Kirov."

Under their pressure he had to stage ballets on contemporary themes, reflecting the victories of the Soviet people in agriculture or space flight. He himself created *Distant Planet* on the space theme which became fashionable after Yuri Gagarin's flight (but the ballet provoked no enthusiasm in America). To my chagrin, I took part in it. But I still don't think that, given his rare professionalism in relation to the classics, Sergeyev really believed in the artistic value of such ballets. He was forced to obey the dictates of his bosses, and it was probably against his will that he included in the repertoire ballets of his friends, such as Zakharov's *Russia Has Come into Port,* about how Soviet sailors are so noble and Western ones are so corrupt. He, who could create *à l'improviste* all kinds of variations or pas de deux in Petipa's pure style, was surely equipped to grasp the real worth of this pedestrian nonsense. But he was a conformist, and put up a good façade. He didn't want to jeopardize his own position. He lived under pressure and simply accepted the rules of the game, squandering the energy of the world's best dancers on this kind of junk.

Thank heaven, my situation as a romantic ballerina did not allow Sergeyev to use me in all of his so-called contemporary ballets. I simply did not fit them.

When I think of Sergeyev's situation at the Kirov, I can even feel sorry for him. Unlike some of my Kirov colleagues who have found themselves in the West, I am not inclined to blame Sergeyev alone for the damage sustained by the best classical company in the world. He, too, was a victim of the whole political system in Russia, his artistic range severely restricted from above. But at least he knew how to maintain the purity of classical dance; those who took his place could not compete with his knowledge and his professionalism. That is why the company began to deteriorate even faster after Sergeyev's dismissal. He was somehow sincere in banning from the Kirov all that did not satisfy his own aesthetic criteria; even in his dislike for the important innovations of Leonid Yakobson, he showed a certain logic and artistic consistency.

In my first year at the Kirov I was fabulously lucky—I fell into the hands of ballet master Yakobson. Stories were told about him at the Theatre, and he had plenty of ill-wishers, not without reason. In the late fifties and early sixties, Yakobson made no attempt to conceal the spirit of rebellious experimentation which had possessed him since the twenties. He sounded a distinctly dissonant note in the hothouse atmosphere of the "citadel of the classical ballet," which is what the Kirov had always been. In

Top: ROMEO AND JULIET *(Lavrovsky)*

Bottom left: SWAN LAKE—*Odile*

Bottom right: SWAN LAKE—*Odette*

Leningrad it was the Maly Theatre that existed as a place for experiments,
but by then it had already turned into a pitiful ruin of itself. Within the
confines of the Kirov, Yakobson's philippics against the classics, which he
openly referred to as the "repulsive trash" of Petipa, Ivanov, Gorsky,
sounded like more than an impassioned reaction to the past. Throughout
his whole life, he had been accused of every possible "ism": eroticism, formalism, surrealism.

Of his full-length ballets, apparently only *Spartacus* was presented in
America, at a time when it had deteriorated completely as a performance.
Of his miniatures, *Vestris* was performed several times in the mid-seventies
by Baryshnikov, *The Blind Girl*, a work created for Shelest's dramatic talent, was seen in the West at the beginning of the sixties. But unfortunately
the choreography of this work suffered from jarring melodrama and looked
dated almost at once. That is why I understand my London friends when
they smile ironically or even express disdain at the mention of Yakobson
and fail to share my enthusiasm for him. Yakobson's innovative works, such
as *The Twelve* or *The Bedbug*, were never shown abroad (no doubt to pre-
vent anyone from suspecting the Kirov of betraying its honored traditions).

Yakobson is absolutely unique. His style brought together, naturally,
pantomime (sharpened almost to the point of graphic art or caricature);
classical and neo-classical elements, shuffled together as cards in a pack;
sculptural gesture; music hall . . . anything at all. All the vocabulary of
ballet was subordinated to one thing—the utmost expressiveness of the
dancer's body, which, he felt, is capable of expressing every emotional nuance or feeling. Each of his ballets created a furore. He was damned on all
sides. By liberal critics for excesses of taste and heavy-handedness—he
did not grasp the concept of "too much." Conservative guardians of classical hygiene were incensed because, in imitating Fokine, he abused turned-
in positions *(en dedans* but not *en dehors)* because his combinations were
frequently unbeautiful from a purely classical point of view. But more than
anything, critics were furious with Yakobson's pose as an *enfant terrible*.
He was notorious for saying whatever popped into his head and, in truth,
he was not modest when it came to himself. He was known as the "Chagall
of ballet," so fertile was his imagination, so original and diverse was his
plastic vocabulary. The analogy with Chagall was particularly striking in relation to his production of Shostakovitch's *Jewish Wedding*, which was suppressed after the first general rehearsal. (Jewish themes are never encouraged on the Soviet stage.)

Most dancers did not like Yakobson. Used to the standard classics, they
felt uncomfortable in his contorted, expressively sharpened poses, which, in
addition to everything else, Yakobson demanded they imbue with emotional
content. Beautiful but sluggish bodies capable only of serving as props on
stage made him furious, and at rehearsals he often tossed off caustic re-

marks to this effect, remarks for which the dancers could not forgive him.

He noticed me at once. "What a sex bomb has turned up," he said to someone behind my back (his words were passed on to me at once). I cannot imagine what he saw in me, although it's true that, at the time, my figure was a lot more rounded than today. My soft legs did not reveal their muscular structure, and all my lines were too flowing and smooth, like those of a romantic ballerina, the role into which I was immediately thrust.

I accepted this role submissively—it would have been flattering for any graduate—although I sensed quickly that I would soon find it confining. Yakobson helped me to realize this, as no one else did.

In 1958, he was working on the ballet *Choreographic Miniatures* and offered me a part in a small number which is a section of the work's *Triptych on Themes of Rodin*. It included three miniatures to music by Debussy: *Eternal Spring*, *The Kiss*, and *The Eternal Idol*—three reflections on various stages of love rendered by animated sculptures of Rodin. *Eternal Spring* was an impromptu piece on the first stage. *The Eternal Idol* dealt with destructive and irresistible passion. *The Kiss* was bathed in the daylight of mature feeling, the highest stage of mutual understanding. The plastic language of these numbers combined the free kinetics of Isadora Duncan and the lexicon of Fokine's old ballets, rendered in the rhythmic medium of the experimentation which had enthralled Yakobson as early as the thirties.

I danced in *The Kiss*, which in its vocabulary tended more than the others toward the classics. An eighteen-year-old girl, I was representing an eternal, quite generalized friend—the constant companion of a man whom I clung to as a protector, an older brother, as if sharing with him my doubts and vexations and hopes. Amazingly, for an eighteen-year-old debutante I "pulled on" that somewhat immodest role like a glove. At the time, I was terribly shy and blushed continuously—from compliments, from confusion, from my halting knowledge of the ballet. Sexually naïve and intrinsically shy, I looked in *The Kiss* like a mature, experienced woman. This was all the more astonishing since in Russia sexual maturity comes rather late. In the Vaganova School we dreamed of love and were stuffed with romantic nonsense. I believe Yakobson may have sensed the sensual suggestions of my movements, the responsive qualities of my body reacting to the music and the erotic overtones of his choreography. I was entirely involved in *The Kiss:* it provided the first opportunity for me to feel on stage what I had not experienced in life. Yakobson soon asked me to dance Zoya Berezkina in his ballet *The Bedbug*, loosely based on Mayakovsky's play of the same name.

Working on *The Bedbug* was a turning point for me—and a creative joy, the kind of thing which was my lot all too infrequently. Yakobson seemed to me like a demigod creating his own, unique theatrical world. What that world would look like at the finale only he knew, and, possibly, even he knew only the outline, the bare bones. He created almost in an in-

Top: COUNTRY OF WONDER

Bottom left: Ravel's WALTZES

Bottom right: BLIND GIRL

p left: THE BEDBUG, *with Konstantin Rassadin*

p right: Leonid Yakobson

ttom: THE BEDBUG, *with Askold Makarov*

spired frenzy, forgetting what had been worked out the day before in the search for something new in the poses and the *mise en scène*. This was exciting for some, but others would get upset. (It is not surprising that, without Yakobson, it is virtually impossible to resurrect many of his ballets; he himself would forget them, enjoying the creative process but cooling toward the final work.)

The ballet of *The Bedbug* was more than a variation on the theme of the play. Yakobson would hardly have been interested by the crass "nepmen," who had long since disappeared from the scene. (The NEP—New Economic Policy—period in the twenties was a time when private property and small business were permitted.) The "nepmen" disappear spontaneously—more likely, undergo spontaneous combustion—in the play by Mayakovsky, who supposed with innocent optimism that there would be no place for them in the newly hatched Soviet paradise. The vitality and cockroach-like durability of the self-satisfied crassness which flourished in the Soviet Union in the succeeding years intrigued Yakobson. He hated these petits bourgeois, smug, militantly ignorant types, akin to the characters in Ionesco's *Rhinoceros*. Essentially, they were the ones—now in their roles as Party bosses and guardians of ideological purity in art—who had forced their retrograde tastes on him and interfered with his realizing his precious talent. He set his satirical sights on them in his *Bedbug*—and without restraint; it took real daring to drag out a huge nuptial bed with a satin blanket onto the puritanical stage at the Kirov and then have my unfaithful love and his new lady squirming about in it, like two gigantic insects, in a love duet. The same is true for the scene of the wedding, with its bottles, cigarette butts, flowers, the fat rear ends wiggling to the chirring of the fox trot and the greasy wedding cortege. The humor was Rabelaisian and the taunts vicious.

Yakobson made Mayakovsky himself the main character of the ballet: the poet was constantly on stage, almost as if creating the performance in front of the audience. He would invoke on the boards images born of his turbulent fantasy, "cross them out," and change the action. He opened up the work of his creative laboratory, as it were. This appeared like a fresh, almost daring experiment, of which there was little enough in the Russian ballet.

Zoya Berezkina is a young, naïve girl who has fallen in love with a self-satisfied dolt who betrays her young feelings: she ultimately checks out of life. Essentially, Yakobson proposed that I re-create the basic lines of my Giselle, though not in a romantic tunic and on pointe, but on low heels, in a faded, ill-fitting little dress, and with a short, boyish haircut. I appeared on stage shaking my shoulders and swinging my hips, and I simply reveled in it—I loved both Zoya's brazenness and her shy vulnerability. At the time, I was not very unlike my heroine and, basically, I danced by myself. This time, Vera Krasovskaya saw in me a "with-it girl" of the sixties. There were plenty of them in Russia, rebelling against their parents' control, girls who seemed ashamed of their girlhood, hiding it under the mask of nihilistic bravado and contempt for all constraints. The choreography of my part called for me to utilize the movements, transformed by Yakobson, of rock and the twist. I did not play a part; I was simply myself and felt no discomfort at being a romantic ballerina who was dancing on heels, with knees knocking, a springy step, awkward lines, and crossed arms. My friends said to me: "So you're eager to distort your beautiful body in those ugly poses!" I loved it, especially my last solo, my "talk with the stars," after my chosen one, Prisypkin—now transformed into Pierre Skripkin—has married the heavyset Elzevir Renaissance. I run about, unaware, as if borne along by unbearable pain, tossing my legs back, knees giving way, dropping, writhing, and clutching with my hands in the air, and cold, indifferent stars are burning high overhead. Then I stop, helpless, and commit suicide, putting my head in an imaginary noose and swinging in the wind.

In *The Bedbug*, I sensed for the first time just how constrained I had felt in the romantic vein. I sensed that I was a lyrical dramatic ballerina; that in ballet I needed some sort of drama, narrative or not, but drama of some kind of turmoil for the soul. Obstacles. Struggle. I am eternally grateful to Yakobson for believing in me and, little by little, as it were incidentally, drawing out my nature and my self. Thereafter, I did not have to coax it out of myself. I was possessed by power. I wanted to try everything, to empty myself into the dance; and somewhat like a good horse, I needed a tight rein. Yakobson simply gave me the chance to get free of constraints and a kind of inexplicable shame that had been preventing me from opening up. Like a skilled puppeteer, he manipulated the strings of the various sides of my nature—my gift, if you will—and I, obediently and joyfully, whirled in his hands.

After *The Bedbug*, Ravel's *Waltzes* followed in 1963, though the work was soon dropped from the repertoire. The waltzes were arranged in the form of pictures in the style of the Second Empire, united by a single theme: the changeable nature of love, its caprices, its ebb and flow. Each waltz had its own story. I danced the second and the seventh, in which the outlines of a drama à trois took shape. In the second, I was an obstinate, touchy, capricious creature with an excessively ardent lover begging for indulgence. In the seventh, I rejected him, not so much in order to find happiness as to find a new focus for my whimsicality in a new love and at the same time to agitate my previous admirer. Although *Waltzes* is not among Yakobson's masterpieces, and while my role was essentially a transitional one, I enjoyed the work each time I danced it. Undoubtedly my pleasure came less from the role itself than from the outlet it gave to the turbulent nature which boiled within me—another instance when the ballet allowed me to experience what had not yet occurred in my own life. I breathed so easily in an atmosphere that provided a free range of feeling, where whim,

63

ELLE, *with Yuri Soloviev*

natural as breathing, was permitted. *Waltzes* (which was soon to fall silent) helped me a few years later to assimilate my Manon so quickly: Yakobson had guided me correctly, as if foreseeing my future roles and preparing me for them.

I sometimes failed to catch this with my intuition and thus lost my chance. It happened with Yakobson's ballet *The Twelve*, after Alexander Blok's important poem. This may have been the most daring of Yakobson's offspring; for 1964 the work was unbelievably audacious. The twelve revolutionary soldiers (in Blok, the twelve Apostles), in the face of a fierce raging wind, did not move toward a white Christ crowned with roses, blessing, as it were, their noble outburst directed at the unjust world, but, instead, against a background of a semi-Cubist set, they seemed to plunge into an abyss, toward the Antichrist, thereby nullifying the creative force that inspired the Russian Revolution.

The powers that be were upset. I was at the preview of *The Twelve*. The Party higher-ups were fuming, most of all over the way the twelve Red Army men passed into the future—not with a sovereign stride befitting soldiers of the Revolution but as if they were Red bedbugs scrambling up a ramp from beyond which blinding scarlet light poured, the glow from the world conflagration. Standing with their backs to the audience, they looked meekly into this future.

Yakobson tried to justify himself before the censors by saying that the future is known to no one and that it is possible only to look into it furtively. "Ah, so you still are unfamiliar with the future of our Revolution?" they asked him threateningly. "*We* are familiar with it." Of course, Yakobson might have tried to maneuver around them, as he had sometimes done, deceiving the Party bureaucrats, many of whom undoubtedly hadn't even read Blok's *The Twelve*. But he persisted and refused to change the finale. Things developed in an almost grotesque manner. A year later, Yakobson had thought up a new ending. He decided to bring on Blok's Jesus Christ with a red banner in his hands, a logical conclusion: who but Jesus ought to lead his apostles? He was to appear from the wings, then disappear like a mirage in front of the Red Army men.

Yakobson's idea was met in the new "artsoviet" with confusion and caustic laughter. "What are you up to? Are you mocking us, Leonid Veniaminovich?" they asked Yakobson. And with that the matter was closed. *The Twelve* was never shown again to the public.

Today, I am very sorry that I did not share with Yakobson the fate of his fallen ballet and did not dance Katka, the slut and whore, the lost soul swept to nowhere by the merciless Revolutionary turmoil, by the wind, by the play of raging elements. Katka's entrance, swinging her hips, stamping her feet provocatively, Yakobson had created for me. I started to rehearse her, but I was overwhelmed with the classic repertoire (at the time, I was struggling with *Swan Lake*) and there was no time or strength left for

Katka. Moreover, I couldn't give myself over entirely into Yakobson's hands. To dance constantly with the feet turned in was physically—stylistically—dangerous. One way or another, I was emerging as a romantic ballerina, and had to assert myself in this mode, which suited the Kirov so perfectly. Yakobson demanded too much involvement and energy from me, and I simply couldn't cope with my double burden, particularly not at the risk of losing my classical form. So I turned entirely to the classics.

With his shortcomings in matters of taste, his overloading of the plastic vocabulary, Yakobson truly despised Noverre's formula for the ballet: "Le Champ des Mesures." The Yakobsonian superfluity overflowed in another of his ballets, *Country of Wonder,* a rather clever stylization of the Palekh masters of lacquer decoration (whose black boxes with brilliantly colorful representations from Russian folklore are bought up by foreigners at the tourist shops). I danced the Beautiful Maiden, whose beloved, performed by Valery Panov, is consumed by fire in an attack by barbarians. I am blinded; then, unseeing, gather his ashes and scatter them to the wind. From the ashes, youths grow. To reveal my love, I am given miraculous vision and the alien devils are driven out.

In this ballet, Yakobson rejected his favorite game of political allusions and retreated into a somewhat naïve, wondrous world of balletic stylization. I liked the atmosphere of fairy-tale primitivism that infused the ballet, but, mainly, it provided me with a role for which I had been yearning. The choreography of the Beautiful Maiden gave me drama and lyricism and the grotesque—everything I have always desired in a role. I remember the marvelous (and basically classical) variation "The Brook," with its brisés, pas de bourrée, and canary-like trembling hands. Just as unforgettable was the monologue on bent knees, with clasped hands, grotesque and reminiscent of Picasso's sculpture. I scattered the ashes of my beloved, and the newly born members of his retinue pressed me upward on their hands. My heart sank from terror—from childhood I had had a fear of heights—as I floated above the raised forest of hands, and prayed to God that this torture would soon pass.

This was my best role with Yakobson, and for it I was named the best Soviet ballerina of the year.

A Passing Beauty, a miniature of Yakobson's after a Picasso motif, was produced for me and presented only twice at the Conservatory that same year, 1967. After the second performance, I got a telephone call from the Party Obkom (the State Party Commander). Some unknown character recommended insistently that I not dance this ballet of Yakobson's "in consideration of my future career."

I did not work with Yakobson after 1967. He had become tired of his position as pariah at the Kirov and had left to organize his own theatre of ballet miniatures. Later, when I found myself in the West, I only heard rumors of his further theatrical innovations, and, as far as I could judge, he

Rehearsing LE CORSAIRE

LE CORSAIRE, *with Yuri Soloviev*

did not create anything essentially new. He needed gifted and attentive performers responsive to his talented will, and, other than Alla Osipenko, who went with him, he had no one worthwhile at his disposal.

In the autumn of 1975 I learned that Yakobson had died of cancer. And I pictured clearly to myself how his coffin must be standing in the large foyer of the theatre, how the eulogies must be sounding saccharine and false about the departure of "an irreplaceable talent, whose contribution . . ." Words spoken by those for whom Yakobson was an impertinent disrupter of their bureaucratic tranquillity. I can imagine what he would have said, if he had been able to speak, in response to their unctuous verbiage.

And today, having worked with Tudor, Robbins, MacMillan, Cranko, and Tetley, I feel a sense of especial bitterness at the waste of Yakobson's potential. In fact, in the works of these talented Western masters, I recognize the turbulent genius of Yakobson—a genius they never saw. After his ballet *Shurale,* at the Kirov they said jokingly: "He's forced the best company in Europe to dance on its ass." But Europe and America hardly knew him. To resurrect, even with films, Yakobson's ballets without Yakobson is impossible. But his lessons are in me, as well as his memory and my unforgettable gratitude.

From my first moment in the Kirov, the Company revealed itself to be more than a collection of merely talented dancers. Almost everyone combined in himself the teachings of the Vaganova School and real artistry. But Dudinskaya and Sergeyev, survivors from the marvelous old guard to which Ulanova, Chabukiani, Semyonova, Yermolaev, and others had belonged, were dancing out their days with all the flaws of decline.

I liked Dudinskaya only in *Don Quixote* and *Laurencia.* She had been brilliantly schooled by Vaganova, and she possessed phenomenal technique—a fabulous soaring jump and all kinds of tours—as well as the most appealing dance energy. Even at fifty-seven she could perform double tours on the diagonal, crossing the Kirov stage at enormous speed. No wonder she was acclaimed as a real virtuoso, trained in the best traditions of the former Maryinsky. As Odette or Aurora she never moved me, because lyricism was entirely alien to her artistic temperament, but her technique remained unmatchable through her final performances on the Kirov stage.

The career of Alla Shelest was also coming to a close. She did not achieve worldwide fame only because the ballet did not travel abroad in her day. A ballerina with exceptional classical schooling, Shelest was controversial in the romantic style, but astonishing in roles with bacchanalian scope, such as Laurencia and as Aegina in Yakobson's *Spartacus,* as well as in parts demanding great dramatic expressiveness. In lyric works like *Giselle* her talent seemed too contrived, affected, almost pathological.

It happened that I studied under Shelest for a whole year, when she became a coach, but I was not able to get anything from her. There were many reasons for this. First, I was never thrilled by her tremendous personality. I felt something artificial in her; something very cold. In addition, as a teacher she usually imposed herself on her students and never took their own individualism into account. I am convinced such methods are entirely wrong. I spontaneously resisted her immense impact and rejected everything. I behaved this way because at that time analyzing or scrutinizing was not my strength; I relied completely on my intuition, my immediate emotional reactions. And because of my resistance, there was no emotional contact between us. Finally, I just didn't *understand* her very knotty and intricate corrections. They really did sound like: "Take your right shoulder through the left but tuck and pass it through the left heel." I was totally confused. Nevertheless, a souvenir of Shelest has remained in my dances—when I do the mad scene in *Giselle,* and my peasant girl, remembering her earlier dance with Albrecht, dances beyond the music, even off the beat. This is my tribute to Shelest, who used to perform Giselle this way.

The last, most gifted students of Agrippina Vaganova had arrived in the Company to replace these *monstres sacrés:* Alla Osipenko, Nelli Kurgapkina, Irina Kolpakova; then the slightly younger Igor Chernyshev and Rudolf Nureyev, who had appeared in the theatre two years before me. Then came our generation: Alla Sizova, Nikita Dolgushin, Yuri Soloviev, Valery Panov. When I think about many of these dancers (not Rudolf, of course), I am overcome by two feelings: irritation and pity. This does not apply to Kurgapkina, who was only a sweet ingenue and did not shine with any particular genius. She became a Party member and duly qualified as a "People's Artist of the USSR." And it doesn't apply either to Kolpakova, who, as one Russian critic noted wryly, took the entire one hundred percent of her potential and made of it three hundred percent. Possessing absolutely no individuality, but a marvelous, totally academic training, Kolpakova became emblematic of the purity of academic dance in the Kirov Theatre. As a professional I can appreciate the virtue of this type of dancing, but it has always left me indifferent, especially in *Giselle,* where a dry, academic approach always seems offensive in relation to the ballet itself, to the unpretentious story of first love, first deception, death, and farewell beyond the grave. Even in *The Sleeping Beauty,* recognized as Kolpakova's greatest role, I always felt a lack of sufficient subtlety, a sort of Soviet disregard for halftones, a lack of that French grace with which I was once struck in Liane Daydé's Giselle.

Alla Sizova distinguished herself not only by her enticing radiance that made her Aurora so special, but also by her extraordinary jump and extension. Her développés à la seconde in the pas de deux from *Le Corsaire,* which she had danced at the graduation performance with Rudolf Nureyev, were simply breathtaking.

Top left: Rehearsing HAMLET *with Konstantin Sergeyev*

Bottom left: Rehearsing CINDERELLA *with Sergei Vikulov*

Bottom right: Rehearsing COUNTRY OF WONDER *with Yuri Ponomarev*

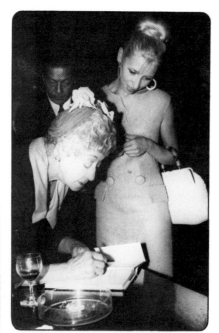

Top left: Natalia Dudinskaya and Konstantin Sergeyev, London

Top right: With Tamara Karsavina

Center right: With Galina Ulanova at Varna

Bottom: With Bronislava Nijinska

But behind the names of Osipenko, Tchernishov, Sizova, Dolgushin, Soloviev, there arises a terrifying picture of spiritual and physical crises, unfulfilled creative promise, and young lives ruined.

The fate of Yuri Soloviev is the most tragic. His life was cut off in a puzzling, almost inexplicable fashion in his thirty-seventh year—a fateful number, fateful for Mayakovsky, for Pushkin, and many others. If one is to believe the stories coming out of Leningrad, Yuri was found dead at his dacha in the winter of 1977: he was lying in his bed under a blanket with a bullet hole in his temple. In his cold hands he clasped his hunting rifle. The windows and doors were closed tightly from the inside, and even a trained investigative eye could uncover no trace of a break-in or attack. What is true and what is fantasy in this story is difficult to tell, especially for me, thousands of miles away from the tragedy. But most probably Yuri committed suicide. And, as always in these cases, there were doubtless many reasons. I will not even attempt to guess at the possible personal ones, but those related to his creative life are all too clear to me.

He was a very special dancer, with a phenomenal ability to leap into the air and seem to hang there. He was impeccably "schooled" and displayed an elegant artistry. But when one thinks about what he truly achieved, only his Blue Bird comes to mind, a role in which he was not equalled in his own day, and probably will not be for a long time to come. Is that not little enough? He was good in *Swan Lake, Giselle, The Sleeping Beauty;* his dancing was always beyond reproach. But no miracle took place—that miracle of the opening of a human personality. There was nothing moving in his execution; he did not astound with his strangeness or extravagance, something to transcend the stereotype.

I do not think that, as a person, he had been deprived of individuality. But no one had worked with him; no one nurtured his soul or fostered his mind; no one ever produced a ballet to tap Soloviev's inner world. This was a Stradivarius which played beautifully, but never sang. Rudi and Mischa had Pushkin; Vasiliev had Yermolaev to pull the individuality out of him. I went though the school of Yakobson. Yuri had no one. And he was too weak to break through to self-realization in isolation.

Moreover, Yuri was well aware that none of the three leading fugitives from the Kirov had perished in the West. On the contrary, he knew we were thriving. He had missed his chance, and surely he was very sorry about that. He was thirty-seven, and the future would bring—nothing. Routine existence, a pension, at best teaching or work as a coach.

Another unhappy fate, though of course less tragic, befell the creative life of my first partner in *Giselle*, Nikita Dolgushin. He had an ideal romantic configuration, superb training—and an intellectual approach which occasionally worked against him. Nikita loved to overload a role like Albrecht with a superabundance of psychological and sometimes far-fetched details.

In Act I, his Albrecht was more like a young brooding Hamlet whose affection for a simple peasant girl seemed to be motivated by strong intellectual curiosity—a testing of his own ability to love. In Act II, he really raged, tossing about on the stage in pursuit of a shadow created by his poetic imagination. He was so deeply involved in his game with the unreal Wili, Giselle, that he almost neglected the real dancer, me, on the stage. He succeeded in evoking the image of some Greek hero driven by demons of fury, but meanwhile the contours of our naïve, romantic drama about love and repentance became blurred and distorted. But none of this was the reason for his downfall. In fact, after Nikita's debut in *Giselle,* people at the theatre started saying that a new Sergeyev had appeared.

This talk and the cries of ecstasy around Nikita presumably were displeasing to the "original." Nikita was saddled with pas de trois, second parts; he was given no solos. Finally, he was given *Giselle* with Alla Shelest, who by then could hardly dance at all, and nothing good came of this for him. In the fall of 1962, he went to Novosibirsk, to the ballet troupe there directed by Oleg Vinogradov. He did very well for a time, then became distressed. His place was at the Kirov, and he returned, at the end of the sixties, to take a sort of examination of artistic maturity to assure himself a place in the Company. In 1968 he danced, wonderfully, *A Legend of Love* with Alla Osipenko, and a *Giselle,* not as successfully, with me. He still over-intellectualized his Albrecht. His fate was decided by the theatre's "artsoviet," which danced to Sergeyev's tune, and Nikita was not taken back into the Kirov. Sergeyev had accused him of being excessively refined (read effeminate) in his manner of execution. I was personally quite disturbed, because with none of my other partners in Russia did I have a relationship so stimulating and so interesting in every respect. Nikita went to the Maly Theatre to work under Igor Belsky and, later, Vinogradov; he danced his Albrecht, the Prince in *Swan Lake, Coppélia,* and *La Fille Mal Gardée.* He did not achieve anything of significance, because no one created for him roles worthy of his talent, and the great promise that he had shown at the beginning of his career remained unfulfilled.

Strangely enough, I don't remember Rudolf Nureyev at the Theatre at all, though apparently we worked side by side there for two seasons ('59 and '60). It somehow happened that I did not see a single production with him. I don't think he was exactly enthusiastic about me in those years; he preferred virtuosi like Xenia Ter-Stepanova, whose dancing looked to me more like exercises in choreographic penmanship. Once, at some sort of critique, he came out against my moving up in the Company ("Why promote her when she can hardly stand up on her legs?"). And he stood up for his own partner, the same Ter-Stepanova. In fact, he remembers my "ill-starred tricks" on the stage of the Kirov better than I do. Just recently, he reminded me how I smeared my face so heavily with make-up, for the sake of greater Spanish swarthiness in *Don Quixote,* that when I placed my

Top: PAS DE QUATRE. *Left to right: Valentina Gannibalova,*
Makarova, Ludmilla Kovaleva, and
Natalia Bolshakova

Bottom left: LENINGRAD SYMPHONY

Bottom right: GORYANKA

Top: DISTANT PLANET

Bottom left: Rehearsing ROMEO AND JULIET *with Anatoly Nisnevitch*

Bottom right: SYRINX

cheek next to Kitri's, it left a spot. And there was Inna Zubkovskaya, truly a beauty, with a dark reddish-brown patch on her peach-colored face, as if she had been burned by a hot iron.

The summer of 1965 was marked by an exciting event: I was invited to take part in the annual international competition of young dancers in Varna. The invitation came as a sudden surprise. Usually this competition demands many months of rehearsing; for me it was an exhausting impromptu. I got a call from Galina Ulanova, who was to preside over the jury in Varna, suggesting that I enter myself in the competition, because there were not very many participants from the Soviet Union. I went to Varna with my partner Anatoly Nisnevitch. We didn't even have enough time to arrange our program, which eventually included the Blue Bird pas de deux from *Sleeping Beauty*, the white adagio from *Swan Lake*, and the balcony scene from Lavrovsky's *Romeo and Juliet*. In addition, Vladimir Tikhonov offered to partner me in the black pas de deux from *Swan Lake*. My program fully corresponded to the requirements of the competition, except for the lack of any contemporary choreographer's piece.

When I recall Varna, I feel almost physically its tremendous heat, the exhaustion of our rehearsals on the open stage under the burning sun. And I recall the wonderful natural sets—the pale blue sky and the dark green verdure of the big trees. Some of my recollections are less pleasant: the hectic atmosphere almost of huckstering, the frenzy, and all the participants concerned only with seeking the maximum number of points. I suppose this atmosphere may be stimulating for very young dancers, for whom it might seem a test of their professionalism, but it can hardly encourage the more developed dancers, of whom I was one. That is why I was not fully satisfied with the Varna competition, although it brought me the Gold Medal. If I passed some test in Varna, it was a test of my inner strength and endurance. I danced in front of a very knowledgeable audience—my judges were Ulanova, Alicia Alonso, and Erik Bruhn. Besides, I got a unique opportunity to become acquainted with the professional level of my Western colleagues.

But probably the most exciting and unexpected experience at Varna came from my work with Ulanova, who committed herself to helping me with my *Giselle* despite her being so tremendously busy. For me it became a real ordeal: my balletic idol was descending from her throne to appear before me in her everyday attire. I was very shy and awkward from confusion and embarrassment, but Ulanova seemed not to notice, and through her rare simplicity finally made me feel natural. Her remarks were utterly precise and never missed their target. I remember one of them, referring to the arabesque penchée at the beginning of the duet in Act II. Ulanova said that this penché doesn't make any sense, because it disrupts the cantilena of the steps. Besides, it is followed by the simple arabesque that seems to exclude the initial penché, since the choreography here should be developing in its intensity. And although I had been doing this penché in accordance with the Kirov tradition, I now stopped. This work with Ulanova was Varna's most lasting benefit to me.

Looking back at my Kirov period, I see that there was a certain logic to it; I danced practically the entire repertoire, so I cannot say that I was "cramped." It is quite another matter that the selection itself was limited. But despite the limitations, I did not often have to dance the "static" ballets, those works devoid of dramatic qualities which I found so boring. Even *Sleeping Beauty* I danced only twice, a role which held little attraction for me at the time. (I was really more interested in dancing Princess Florine than Aurora, because Florine's style demands a special purity. It excludes improvisation, strictly adhering to academic patterns, and in addition it requires a highly refined elegance which has to be in your very blood.) Twice, I performed Vainonen's academic and monotonous *Nutcracker*.

I danced very little in the so-called Soviet ballets, falsely motivated, very *terre à terre,* and often simply nonsensical. They were supposed to be included in the repertoire as daily fare. (In Russia, even the ballet is supposed to reflect the nation's success, space flights, up-to-date reality—quite incompatible with the abstract nature of ballet.) Even in a ballet like Igor Belsky's *Leningrad Symphony,* far from being the worst example of Socialist Realism, I felt myself out of place. At times, I was ashamed to come out on stage—the choreography was so ridiculous. It would seem that the music of Shostakovitch and the theme itself—the blockade of Leningrad, the horrors of the Nazi invasion, which touched my life directly—could be in no way nonsensical, but I felt ridiculous with all the marching, leaping young men in tights representing German soldiers, the girls doing pas de bourrée and stupidly waving their arms. I only liked the violent scene, but I couldn't bear to get down on my knee with a weapon at the ready—the gesture was too ordinary, not removed enough from reality, and therefore false. And this falseness sickened me. I felt the gesture to be alien to ballet in general. (How odd that if it had been a bow and arrow in my hands, I would have felt nothing of the kind.)

The Party administration which oversaw the Kirov did not understand that it is impossible to produce a ballet about the construction of a hydroelectric plant. Not long ago, in the Bolshoi, Yury Grigorovich created a ballet like that, *Angara,* and even without seeing it I'm absolutely sure that it cannot be any good. The opening up of virgin lands, as well as dancing with a machine gun or going to the bathroom or representing an abortion, are just as impossible in ballet. Things have not come to such extremes as abortion, but in *Native Fields* there was a meeting of a Party Committee on the Kirov stage; rifles and machine guns were used at the Maly in *Youth;* and a tractor appeared in *Asel,* on the Bolshoi's stage. Such well-intentioned nonsense was not done out of ignorance, but from a serious failure to understand the nature of ballet, an art which is extremely dependent on conventions, in which everyday details can play a role only when you extract from them their poetic essence.

I did not like Sergeyev's ballets—not *The Path of Thunder*; not *A Distant Planet*; not *Cinderella*; not *Hamlet*, which I only rehearsed and never performed. In the case of *Cinderella*, my discomfort cannot be explained merely by the insufficiency of Sergeyev's choreography. Frankly speaking, I don't feel any affinity either with the theme or with the music. Probably the simplicity of dramatic conflict hampered my imagination: as a fairy tale, Cinderella always seemed to me too one-dimensional. As for Prokofiev's music, it never sounded danceable or natural to me; only alien.

When Sergeyev revived his *Cinderella*, a piece from the forties, he believed that he was carrying on the work of Petipa, whose style he revered, rejecting everything beyond it. I recall one conversation with him, in a car, on the ballets of Gogi Aleksidze, a young choreographer whose style was slightly reminiscent of Jerry Robbins. "All this reaching for what's fashionable, this decadence, it's all derivative, it'll pass, but Petipa will remain," Sergeyev said, in response to my ecstatic remarks about Gogi.

But his *Cinderella* in the key of Petipa turned out to be simply old-fashioned. I am not actually opposed to the old-fashioned—it can be pleasant and touching, as long as there is some kind of charm or a certain dramatic quality in it. But how could his doll-like Cinderella touch me? She was like a porcelain statuette, and the choreography was smothered in sickly sweetness. Fortunately, Sergeyev at first assigned me the role of Krivliaka (Affected Person), one of the ugly sisters. (Contrary to the Western tradition, in Russia the sisters are never danced by men.) The role was fun; I was able to fool around to my heart's content, dancing a crotchety girl, self-satisfied and spoiled by over-zealous parental care. In a certain way, Krivliaka reminds me of Lise in *La Fille Mal Gardée*, a role I was to dance with ABT six years later. There is one difference: as Krivliaka, I was carried away with quirkiness, and today I would not dance her that way. One of the traits of my character was then emerging—capricious obstinacy, which I think (I hope) I have lost with the years. Vera Krasovskaya, as if looking intuitively into my future, wrote that sometimes my positions on pointe recalled a garish silhouette from the cover of an American detective story (in spite of the wig and farthingale), and that my Krivliaka was just right for sitting in the bar of a transatlantic liner sipping a cocktail.

But if Krivliaka was a fine pretext for fooling around on stage, then the part of Cinderella, which I danced for the first time on tour in Chicago in 1964, was simply boring. A certain asexual quality, something nobly long-suffering, all that bother with the pots in the first act, the quarrels with the sisters and stepmother which are supposed to show how enviably obedient Cinderella is—it was all merely tiring and annoying. The only bright spot

CRELLA (as Ugly Sister)

left: With Ninel Kurgapkina

right: Curtain call with Irina Utretskaya and Kaleria Fedicheva

in the ballet was that moment when love for the Prince awakens within Cinderella. In general, I like best everything that comes before love, the very process of the birth of feelings of love; which is no doubt why I am best at conveying languor and the mounting temperature of love in the dance.

Unlike many of my colleagues at the Kirov, I never suffered from any kind of tyranny. Undoubtedly this was because I tried to avoid conflict: I feared the possibility of humiliation more than anything. In Russia, we all lived under the constant threat of humiliation, since, as in every totalitarian state, we were zeros in the calculations of the higher powers. They could insult us, trample on us as people, abase us, and there was no one we could complain to; the law protects its interests only. In the Theatre I was meek, demanding nothing, never getting hysterical in the office of Piotr Rachinsky, an ex-fireman, whose all-powerful Party card blanketed the Directorate at the Theatre. I never demanded trips abroad from him or a free apartment, as many did, not without success. For three years, I lived in a real closet, without a bathroom, where there was only a bed and suitcases, piled to the ceiling. There, I gave my feet baths in a basin before rushing to a performance.

By not asking anything of Rachinsky, I kept myself from the danger of being humiliated. I did not grumble and, to be truthful, I didn't even feel burdened by my lack of freedom, since I lived in my own internal, isolated world. At this time, with the coming to power of the former fireman, cloddishness became the norm in human relations at the Theatre. At any moment, anyone might burst out with some abusive crudity. And I did not want to engage in any wrangling with anyone ("to assert myself"), since speaking with them in their cloddish language—they understood no other—meant to lower oneself to their uncivilized level. I preferred to grit my teeth; my meekness was a certain self-defense.

I rebelled only once, when I was asked to make the film of *Swan Lake* which was later seen in the West with Elena Evteyeva. The director turned out to be a terrible nonentity who had no taste whatever. I looked at some of the filmed material and was horrified: it was a tasteless production, pure frippery, with some kind of clouds wafting around tiny swans. More important, the director understood nothing about ballet, having previously filmed only some Russian fairy tales for children. He undertook to teach me how to dance Odile: "Dance as if you wanted to seduce me." At this point I lost patience. "I haven't the slightest desire to do that to you," I said, and walked off the set. I refused point-blank to go back on—let others work with this blockhead. Dudinskaya and Sergeyev threw themselves at me: "Have you gone out of your mind? To pass up a chance like this! Who put you up to it?" Later, some clod from the Party Committee called and said in the crass, familiar manner these types usually use: "What sort of manners do you call that, sweetie? Where did you get your education? You've been offered a great honor. . . ." But I wouldn't give in, and I was terribly proud that I did not, in spite of all the threats and admonitions.

After the scandalous incident with *Swan Lake,* I became involved in a new work, *Mozartiana,* which was staged for me by Gogi Aleksidze, and later in his ballet *Syrinx.* Gogi (who is now the chief choreographer of the Tbilisi Ballet, having replaced Vakhtang Chabukiani) was a good person and a fine choreographer, but his talent unfortunately was only for the one-act ballet or the elegant miniature. Of course I was overjoyed to work with him, as the routine had become more and more burdensome—I had been touring abroad a lot, dancing the seventh waltz from *Les Sylphides* or fragments from *Swan Lake.* Oleg Vinogradov put me into his *Mountain Girl* along with Mischa Baryshnikov, whose career at the Kirov was advancing rapidly. But this ballet brought me no joy; the choreography was artificially complex, and there was really no female character at all. I was in a state of complete ennui.

I was saved by Igor Tchernishov, who suggested that I work with him on a long pas de deux to Berlioz' symphonic poem *Romeo and Juliet.* From the first rehearsal I became immersed in the role. The pas de deux (which I danced with Vadim Gulyayev) was essentially a mini-ballet, almost twenty minutes long, which told the story of Romeo and Juliet through the prism of romantic art. It was pure neo-classicism, dynamic, expressive, in which the psychological drama of the lovers from Verona was closely observed. All feelings were examined as if under a magnifying glass; everything breathed of passion, of despair turning into tragic hopelessness.

With the appearance of Baryshnikov in the Company, Igor decided to turn it into a full one-act ballet, since he saw Mischa as an ideal Mercutio. We rehearsed the Berlioz like madmen, by fits and starts, in our rare free moments. To dance Tybalt, Tchernishov called on Valery Panov, whom the role fit perfectly, although he later dropped out. This was a marvelous time. I came alive; in Juliet there was everything that I had longed for at that time: the dramatic flow of robust, active choreography.

When we held a preview, Igor's ballet produced a bombshell. My dear Marietta Frangopolo, with whom I had been friends since school, announced that "this flower of evil must not be permitted to blossom." Dudinskaya and Sergeyev, upon whom the fate of Igor's offspring depended, accused Tchernishov of imitating the West, of formalism, eroticism, and so on. In the heat of the discussion, Sergeyev even went so far as to state that there were Soviet arabesques and Western ones, and that Tchernishov's were exclusively Western—therefore unnecessary to the Soviet public. On the spot they forbade the ballet. Igor and the rest of us were psychologically devastated. It would have been pointless to protest, and I again withdrew into myself, dragging along as before.

Soon I was getting ready to go on tour to London. Irina Kolpakova, thanks to her Party card and connections in high places, took over Tchernishov's *Romeo and Juliet* for herself and managed to get permission for a single performance of it. Before leaving for London, I watched a rehearsal with Kolpakova and Gulyayev and wept from the hurt. . . .

And this is my last recollection of the Kirov. I left for England with a heavy heart, fed up with the repertoire, in despair because the Berlioz had fallen through for me. Frantic boredom and weariness were building up inside me. I felt like starting over again with everything, but I didn't know where or how to begin and struggled to drive away my gloomy thoughts. My thirtieth year was drawing close, but it did not portend any changes.

DANCING IN THE WEST

This time in London, the Kirov's third visit, we were booked to perform at the Festival Hall. I was scheduled to dance *Giselle*. My present Giselle had been born here nine years before, and had gained recognition, which may be why I always had particularly warm feelings for London. At that time, in the summer of 1961, *Giselle* came to me unexpectedly. Rudi had been prepared as a surprise for the British, and after he defected, the Kirov had to show off somebody fresh in order to muffle the noise surrounding him. Sergeyev and Dudinskaya, both about fifty, had decided to fill the gap in *Giselle* themselves, but this insane idea was opposed in the Soviet Embassy. So the choice for New Sensation fell upon me. I discovered these details only recently; I was really puzzled then as to why they would let me undertake such an important performance after a few rehearsals (this was only my third *Giselle*), considering that I was unprepared.

The fact is that in Paris, on the eve of the London trip, I had left some curling pins too long in my hair and burned it; it came out in clumps, and so I arrived in England looking like a *garçon parisien*. They made up some sort of blondish wig for me, got costumes ready (it all was impromptu), and, having slapped everything together, I went on stage. To top things off I got a toothache and my cheek swelled up. So when my first *Giselle* in the West was greeted enthusiastically, it was an unexpected joy for me. Because of all the excitement, I don't even remember how I danced; I only recall that people crowded in the wings and everyone was congratulating Dudinskaya and Sergeyev on their new debutante. . . . That had been a real success, and now, many years later, in 1970, I did not want to disgrace myself. My experience had grown; I had entered the period of my artistic maturity, and more was required of me. Moreover, I had to erase from the memory of the British a vexing incident which occurred during my second appearance in London, in 1966 at the Albert Hall, when—in *Giselle* again—I fell down flat dancing the pas de deux in the second act. My partner, Onoshko, stood over me, as if in a boxing ring, counting: "One, two, three . . . out."

Yet, in spite of my increased responsibility, I was calm, and at the dress rehearsal I just fooled around with Yuri Soloviev, feeling that all that mattered was to extend myself for the performance itself. I was relying on my spontaneity and felt myself mature and free—capable of the role's insanity and any kind of desperate experimentation on stage. And the performance went well.

The month in London was full: as well as *Giselle* I danced a series of classical pas de deux. But, in my soul, I rested. After the upset of the preceding months, London seemed like a safety valve to me.

At that time my attitude, both mental and emotional, to the Western world was somehow different, as if my former impressions from the West, accumulated throughout nine years, had now come into focus.

During my numerous tours I viewed the West mostly from the tourist bus, with the eyes of a foreign ballerina, travelling like Alice in Wonderland. Western life seemed to me more intense, opulent, and diverse than Soviet realities. Its variety in everything, starting with balletic styles and ending with material goods, was always very tempting for me. In Leningrad I often discussed the advantages of Western life with my friends—we talked about a "citizen of the world" position, personal enterprise, freedom in choosing a religious or artistic creed. I was very impressed by some striking balletic personalities, such as Maurice Béjart and Roland Petit, whose productions looked anything but drab. In August of 1970 in London I enormously enjoyed the performances of the American Ballet Theatre, which reinforced my belief in the development of Western ballet.

In short, during that tour in London I felt much more familiar with the exciting, though still alien, world. But I also knew that like a child in the pastry shop, I was allowed to enjoy these Western sweets only temporarily. The idea of remaining for good in this world that wasn't my own never crossed my mind.

Throughout August, I was with English friends all the time, forgetting about restrictions, enjoying myself at parties. I got money from the Kirov to buy a car and, toward the end of the engagement, received a certificate from the Soviet Embassy to obtain the necessary foreign exchange. But always, I found myself thinking about the return to my homeland with a kind of foreboding. It was as if, soon, the ball would be over, the clock would strike, and Cinderella would find herself back in the workaday world. Everything felt strange. At times I was very distressed, and completely indifferent to the future. I felt myself split away from the other dancers, with whom I spent little time, since my English friends were of much more interest to me, nor was I ever concerned about whether or not I would get into trouble for this later on. And even in my manner of dress, for all the limitations of means, an uncharacteristic extravagance appeared. Certain convergences of circumstances that seemed insignificant at the time now look like signs or indicators of the future course of events. So it was, for instance, that I was not invited to a party at Alicia Markova's or Margot Fonteyn's (I don't recall which) because Nureyev was supposed to be there. Instead, after the performance I went for a walk around the city. Heading for the Strand Palace Hotel, I ran into Rudi. Neither of us was surprised at this meeting. A relaxed conversation started up. "I thought you were at the party." "Oh, no, I'm going to a movie." He said something about the lighting being wrong in *La Bayadère*—in short, the talk continued about everyday matters, as if we had seen each other the day before. But actually since our last meeting long years had elapsed. And we parted just as matter-of-factly. At that moment neither he nor I foresaw our future performances together, our tiffs, and our subsequent friendship.

Top left: London, just after defection, 1970

Top right: Televised BLACK SWAN, 1970

*Bottom: London, just before defection: Alla Osipenko,
Mikhail Baryshnikov, Alla Sizova, Makarova, Yuri Soloviev*

And how amusing—and, now, how seemingly significant—the conversation I had with Mischa Baryshnikov in a car taking us to our hotel. I got out first.

"So, don't disappear," he called out in parting.

"And if I do, will you follow me?" I asked him jokingly.

"To the ends of the earth," he answered.

And four years later he turned up in this part of the world. But the possibility of such things happening never entered my mind at that time, although something unforeseen and invisible was coming together around me, a thickening atmosphere fraught with explosive change.

At the end of August 1970, we had a day off, and our friends the Bentons invited the entire company to their country place outside London. But friends had invited me to go horseback riding, for the second time in my life. (It was before a performance of *Les Sylphides* that I rode for the first time. I was so enchanted by riding that, instead of my partner—a romantic poet in a powdered wig—I saw a horse's face that evening. Even soaring in his arms in the seventh waltz, I involuntarily felt a horse's croup between my legs. It was terribly distracting, but I could not get away from the delusion, no matter how I tried.) I warned our hosts that I would arrive late with my English friends, the Rodziankos. We had been introduced by someone from television and had an immediate sympathy for one another. During this trip to London I was especially bold—dining out, going wherever I wanted without informing our KGB snoops—so much so that Piotr Rachinsky, who always treated me nicely, whispered to me: "Tell them beforehand, or they'll be upset." But I didn't pay any attention to him.

When we finally arrived at the Bentons', I saw the whole Company drinking, talking—looking at me askance—and I immediately felt a strange alienation. I even thought, "How curious! I have much more in common with my English friends than with my fellow dancers." When everyone began getting ready to go home, Irina Kolpakova beckoned me to come closer and said, "Natasha, you've got to return to the hotel in the bus with the rest of us." I answered, "I came with friends. It would be impolite. What could I tell them?" Kolpakova added, "They just asked me to warn you." So I apologized to the Rodziankos and made my way toward the bus like a beaten dog. Everything was seething inside me; I felt humiliated for no reason, over nothing. Apparently, my feelings were reflected in my expression, because someone suddenly clapped me on the shoulder and said, "Forget it, forget it, it'll be okay."

I sat there, thinking: "This is the way it will always be. Why should I put up with it?" I bit my lip from helplessness, and that evening lay down to sleep, depressed.

Several days went by, and on September 3 I had no performance. I spent the day running around to the stores. Toward supper time, I set off for the Festival Hall with a huge edition of Salvador Dali, whom I loved at

the time. I wanted to put this tome, a gift from Terry Benton, with my theatre baggage. Everything had been taken care of for departure, including
the canned goods with which Soviet dancers always travel in order to save
some of the small amount of money allotted to us. Since I was eating out
with friends every evening, I had already given away all the food I had
come with. That particular evening I was dining with the Rodziankos at
their home.

In the elevator, going downstairs, I met our dear old KGB agents coming after me (I don't know whether they were spying on me or not), along
with Dudinskaya. Neither of us suspected that we were seeing each other
for the last time. She was pleasant to me as always, and showed me some
photographic proofs of the ballets, saying: "That one's good, but this one
isn't." I was absent-minded and hardly listened; then, leaving, I circled the
theatre for some reason. Only then did I head for the Rodziankos' car. As
if I was covering my tracks. Why? What crime had I committed?

At dinner the conversation didn't jell at first; we talked about this and
that. Then, suddenly, without warning, Irina Rodzianko launched into a
long monologue to the effect that I was destroying myself, that I ought to
fight back and remain in London. In answer, I burst out laughing: "That's
impossible. Let's talk about music instead." Her words came as a surprise,
but although the idea of defecting had never seriously crossed my mind, I
wasn't entirely taken aback. Yes, there was my mother, the Kirov stage,
Leningrad, my friends; the idea of leaving all that was nonsense. And yet
years later my London friends assured me that it had been their clear
impression that I had already thought out my decision to remain.

When I look back, the very fact that I defected in 1970—neither earlier nor later—seems to me rather meaningful. I had had many chances
before, because of my constant tours abroad, on some of which I even trav-
elled alone. So *why* didn't I defect earlier? The only explanation that comes
to me is that throughout my life, everything seems to have occurred *despite*
my conscious plans and projects, rather than in obedience to them. I'm a
fatalist by nature, with a strong belief in predestination. I am motivated by
my emotions rather than by my reason, and as if acknowledging this particular trait of mine, destiny takes the initiative and makes my decisions for
me, only demanding that I say "yes" at the right moment. It was at the
Rodziankos' place that the right moment came, and I responded subconsciously—and affirmatively—to destiny's call. All I had to do was submit
myself to the circumstances—which is why, when I was asked later on
where I had found the courage to defect, I wasn't able to answer. It had
nothing to do with courage. It was resignation to something unavoidable,
imposed upon me as if from above. That was why I was not afraid of the
responsibilities of my decision, or of any of the consequences: it was simply
inevitable.

At a dinner at Anton Dolin's, a few days before, I answered somebody's
question about my future plans with: "What plans! I'll just toil on until I re-
tire. Nothing good is going to happen." Weren't all my doubts and inten-

tions concealed behind those words? Nothing of the kind! That was simply the way I felt; I had no idea at all of defecting. But when at the Rodzian-kos', Irina came back to the attack, her words so convincing, I did not rebel. The thought flashed through my brain: "What if . . ." All my con-fused feelings seemed to come into focus, urging me to do it, and I knew that my hour had struck. It was so painful that I began sobbing hysteri-cally. I cried for some fifteen minutes, I think, as my twenty-nine years rushed through my mind at incredible speed. The whole earlier part of the evening suddenly seemed to me a kind of prophetic dream: the KGB agents in the elevator, coming after me as if spying on me; Dudinskaya, showing me photographs of my ballets; my highly untypical carefulness, making me circle around the theatre before heading for the Rodziankos' car. . . . Everything seemed to have been moving toward some crucial moment that I now was ready to face. And then it happened. Just as abruptly as I had be-gun to weep, I calmed myself and said firmly: "Call the police. I am ready."

Now it was my friends' turn to get upset, and mine to try to calm them. Vladimir Rodzianko was trembling. The situation was becoming ridiculous. I kept saying, "Don't be upset, friends, everything will be okay." At that moment, I remembered that I had left my talisman in the make-up room— a little teddy bear which the Rodziankos' son had bought for me with his own money. I could leave behind anything on earth but this present, which had preserved me from all harm for seven years (and which recently I gave to my friend and coach Elena Kittel-Tchernishova. Let him serve her now; she needs him more than I do.) My friends got a cellist to go into the the-atre at night and steal my treasure. It was time to call the police.

I have gone into such detail here because there have been so many ri-diculous rumors on this subject, rumors which are still making the rounds in Russia. For instance, that I was made drunk or given a knockout shot and dragged to a police station unconscious. No. Two young police officers arrived and asked me if my decision was final, and, having received an af-firmative answer, they took me under their protection. It's strange that these two young men, complete strangers, inspired more trust in me than my own colleagues from the Kirov. They took me to a police station, where I smoked what seemed like ten packs of cigarettes. Permission to remain in England came in the morning.

It goes without saying that there was a commotion in the Company, an immense scandal; it was like a clap of thunder for everyone. My dresser, Valechka, who was very fond of me, took it quite hard. She got drunk and kept sobbing, "Who could have thought that Natashka, our Natashka, is staying. Everybody thought it would be Baryshnikov, but look how it turned out!" My materialistic colleagues were struck more than anything by the fact that I had just purchased a car in England, which I'd now have to abandon. The car was a decoy, many of them decided. But this is the point: I didn't think of a thing ahead of time, didn't make any calculations, but simply acted according to an inner voice.

I was inundated with letters filled with persuasion, flattery, and promises to forget the whole incident if I would only reconsider and return. Sergeyev even remained in London, hoping to meet with me and bring the stray lamb to reason. I got three letters from him. Here is the first:

7 September 1970, London

Dear Natasha,

I am writing to you for the first time and for the first time I have a request for you: to see you and to speak with you. Our troupe has left for Holland. I have stayed in London especially for our meeting. You can understand what sort of state I am in. You cannot refuse, since you know how I feel about you, and you yourself have spoken about mutual feeling, my dear Ophelia. Till we meet soon,

Konstantin Sergeyev

I received the letters through Scotland Yard, which got them from the Soviet Embassy, so I did not for a moment believe in their sincerity. And even if they had been sincere, what would they change? I had taken a decision, and there was no place to retreat—there was only Moscow and all that that implies. I simply wrote to him:

Dear Konstantin Mikhailovitch,

I would love to say many kind and sincere words to you, to reassure you, but I know quite well that at this moment it's beyond my power. Your state of mind is understandable and moves me very much. But the only thing I can do now is to attempt to persuade you that I made my decision without any external influence and that it is firm. I have realized that I really value only one thing in my life, and that is my art. I sacrifice a great deal by taking this decision, but I have to use all my inner resources to realize myself fully in ballet and to say through my dancing everything I feel in my soul and am endowed with. As a real artist, about whom I don't for a minute harbor any doubt, you ought to understand me. I pray to God that in your heart you wish me success.

Thank you for all you did for me, remaining your sincerely loving

Natasha Makarova, as ever

In answer, another letter arrived, written on September 9:

Natasha,

Once more I turn to you with an insistent request that you meet with me. Your answer to my letter was extremely surprising. . . . I am sure that much is being concealed from you and that your answers are being dictated to you. . . . It is as if someone else has been substituted for you; you have become tough and hardhearted. I do not recognize you in this, and I do not want to. I address the Natasha Makarova dear to our heart, whose fate is not a matter of indifference to us and in whose success there is no small portion of our cares and labor and love. Without a meeting, I cannot return to Leningrad. . . . I don't even know whether you are in good health. Whether you are alive? And what is happening with you? It's improbable and incomprehensible that I cannot get to meet with you. It is extremely suspicious, and I am sure that it is coming not from you. I urgently request that, upon receipt of this letter, you inform me of the time and place of our meeting. Impatiently,

Konstantin Sergeyev

I had to send another letter disillusioning him. And I understood that he was worried about himself first of all, and about his post, which he was in danger of losing because he had let down his Soviet guard. Sergeyev was right to worry, since shortly after the defection he really was removed. My flight was the last straw. He was trying to save himself in his third letter, written on September 11. By this time, he had sunk to open demagoguery.

Natasha,

I read your letter with a bitter feeling. Deep sorrow and terrible doubts for your fate possessed me. It would have been possible for me not to answer it. But I have known you too long and too well in order to share your illusions—you have gone far astray and you are not right in your decision. History tells us of something else: when someone is torn from his native roots, he perishes. Natasha, before it is too late, reconsider. Shake yourself free of this delusion. I could tell you many things in a personal meeting, concentrating on the facts of your creative work and being well acquainted with the reality surrounding it. But I do not wish to do so in a letter which will pass through strange hands. I continue to hope for the clearing of your reason and for a meeting with you soon.

Konstantin Sergeyev

I did not answer this letter, since there was nothing to say to it. Why mention those earlier expatriates, Stravinsky, Nabokov, Pavlova, Balanchine—or Nureyev? As opposed to the fate of those who remained—Pasternak, Mandelstam, Akhmatova. We were speaking different languages.

But most striking was the language of another letter—from my dear coach, Tatiana Vecheslova, the "director" of my first roles at the Kirov. "Your not returning home is monstrous. Do you really think any foreigner could respect you? And how would an Englishman look upon someone who had left his homeland? Such people will never see real happiness, regardless of fame and money, for they have infringed the greatest trust: they have betrayed their land. . . ." She continued in the same spirit, as did Alla Osipenko in *her* letter: "It is impossible to believe what has happened. . . . Your soul is Russian. It will not survive what you are doing." Meanwhile, my soul was more or less at peace; somehow it was looking into the future almost unperturbed.

I was taken to a house outside London where I had nothing to do. I gathered mushrooms, walked in the forest accompanied by a very fine gentleman from Scotland Yard; I started to study English again. It was there, in my seclusion, that I wrote a long article about myself, the Theatre, the School, about how precious they are to me and how much they gave to me, about how I am eternally indebted to them, and how my decision had nothing whatever to do with politics. The article, intended for the *Daily Telegraph,* unfortunately did not get onto the newsstands—some sort of strike was going on—and my "last and final confession" was made in vain.

I remained in the West because I did not want to die an early death as a ballerina in the Kirov's routine, which nothing was going to change. For nearly a year I said this over and over, giving interviews all over the world. After all, I was the first refugee from the Leningrad ballet since Rudi Nureyev's memorable flight.

An avalanche of interviews overwhelmed me upon my return to London. They were terribly difficult for me: in twelve years in Russia I hadn't given a single one. And I was not able to speak out openly this way, with an unknown world lying ahead and, behind me, Russia, whose unseen presence I felt constantly, to say nothing of my fear for my mother, my relatives, and friends. I felt constrained and tongue-tied, and was surprised that I could put together even a few sentences for Vladimir Rodzianko to translate.

I cannot say that I lost my head, but it was strange to see my photograph everywhere. The papers were plastered with it. I made no plans: I assumed that something would turn up. There were a few opportunities, nothing major; I danced *The Dying Swan* on London television. And then Rudi and I decided to do the black pas de deux from *Swan Lake*. I didn't relish the idea, since I was still more apprehensive about Odile and her fouettés than about anything else. Yet I agreed—the chance was too good to pass up. I was nervous, and the TV show did not go especially well, though Rudi was all attention and tried to keep my spirits up and support me in every way. I only regret that I did not rise to the occasion and that the tape remains as a kind of eternal reproach. Dancers cannot afford to show such carelessness toward themselves—such concrete evidence, however accidental, can come back to plague us later on, and there is nothing we can do about it.

My plans were unclear, though I hoped that I would be offered a place in the Royal Ballet, which I had loved since the Company's first performances in Russia. But no offer came; I heard that one of the leading ballerinas had announced to the artistic director, "If you hire Makarova, I'm leaving." She did not wish to share her roles with me. I understand: a ballerina's life is short, and everyone wants to realize her potential totally. And the old saying, "Don't expect compliments from a rival," is true more often than not, although happily there are exceptions, instances of altruism, artistic integrity, concern only for art and not for self.

Of course, I didn't know my way around. At a dinner for Frederick Ashton at Rudi's, I simply asked Ashton directly to put something on for me. It's so natural in Russia for a ballerina to do that, and I wasn't one of the most aggressive by any means. I didn't see anything wrong with my request, but I noticed how Svetlana Beriosova raised her eyebrows, apparently shocked at my effrontery. Then I realized I had made a faux pas. So I had my first lesson: I was no longer on my home ground and I would have to learn new rules. In any case, no association with the Royal developed until a year later, when they invited me to perform at a gala for the Queen.

But the American Ballet Theatre invited me to work with them; they were the first to send a telegram. I had heard flattering things about that company. They had toured in the Soviet Union, and Erik Bruhn and Lupe Serrano had created a sensation with the hypercritical Russian audience. I hadn't seen any of their performances, since I was on tour myself somewhere, but I was struck by the variety of the ABT repertoire, of styles and personalities. My original impression had been confirmed during the Company's summer engagement in London, where I was immediately enthralled with Antony Tudor—*Lilac Garden, Pillar of Fire*—with his dramatic expressiveness, warmth, and in particular the subtlety of psychological nuance (for which, at the time, I was quite desperate). The atmosphere of the purely neo-classic works, which I had not danced, was refreshing, and I wanted very much to perform them, especially after the English premiere of Jerry Robbins' *Dances at a Gathering*, which I saw at Covent Garden. I loved Jerry's work at once, and this too encouraged me to go overseas, to America, which I knew only from the 1964 Kirov tour.

In the fall of 1970, I arrived in New York, trunks stuffed with piano scores and books. My first job in America was simply to survive; there was no time even to think about whether I liked it or not. I had changed the scenery of my life and started over from the very beginning. On the one hand, this was easy: I have a carefree nature. I can say good-bye to the past without difficulty and never go back to it; it becomes curtained off, almost unreal. Of course, I missed my parents although I was able to speak regularly to them on the telephone, but that unhealthy nostalgia which usually accompanies psychological transplanting did not cause me any particular suffering.

On the other hand, life was very difficult, since I had never before had to assert myself either as a person or as a ballerina. Rumors made their way to me from Russia: "Natalia is dying there. With her head in the clouds and all her impracticality, she won't be able to stand the tempo or the competitive life." In this there was an element of truth: I am truly not a very practical person, and I don't understand much about financial matters, since that side of life never touched me in Russia. So it is not surprising that during my first two years in America my expenses exceeded my income. But that is not the point.

I understood that I had to demonstrate to everyone that I was, first of all, capable of surviving. For a woman alone in the West, especially in America's male-oriented society, it is significantly more difficult than for a man. Moreover, I was in linguistic isolation, dependent on Vladimir Rodzianko, my interpreter and my manager, who decided and did everything for me. For a long time I did not even know how to make a call from a phone booth, and in my countless interviews I barely understood what the interviewer was asking and what my interpreter was saying in response. I frequently spoke in clichés and was even more boring than I might otherwise have been.

Moreover, almost everyone expected me to abuse the Soviet Union, but I had no desire to criticize my country, since I harbored no ill will against it. My personality was reflected in these interviews incompletely and tangentially, and I didn't make use of the chance I was given as a Russian defector to speak out.

These interviews at first cost me a fiendish amount of effort, and I realized that I was also in psychological isolation. American friends appeared later, and only some time after that a Russian balletic culture sprang up: friends from the Kirov Theatre and School left Russia too. But in 1971, I was entirely alone, and my only outlet was my work.

As I have said, it was the variety of ABT's repertoire that attracted me, and I, who had not danced anything new since 1968, threw myself at all their ballets like a starving person at a table laden with food, paying no attention to how things taste. Sober evaluation came later.

In addition to my constant companions, *Giselle* and *Swan Lake,* I took part in Tudor's ballets *Pillar of Fire* and *Lilac Garden, Romeo and Juliet* and *Dark Elegies.* I rehearsed things completely new to me: *La Sylphide, Coppélia,* and *La Fille Mal Gardée,* Alvin Ailey's *The River, The Miraculous Mandarin,* and others. For my debut at ABT, I chose *Giselle.* Their production greatly differed from the one I was accustomed to: the pantomime was riddled with realistic details, and unusual emphasis was given to the action. Besides, it was my first real experience of working with a Western company (before that I had only danced *Giselle* with a Dutch company in Amsterdam) and I feared getting mixed up in a production whose logic seemed alien to me and to which I could not adjust. I altered certain aspects, attempting to portray my own Giselle, less earthbound, depicted impressionistically, and rather stylized. I was nervous, I rehearsed under great tension because I was not in top form, and therefore I was mostly concerned with the technical aspects of the role.

My partner was scheduled to be Erik Bruhn, an ideal Albrecht to my taste, an elegant and refined stylist. Unfortunately, on the eve of the performance he suffered a serious injury and my Giselle was left without her imaginary fiancé. Taking into account that I also was having difficulties with my too mundane peasant girl's costume, it was the perfect moment to panic.

But at this moment appeared my Prince Charming—Ivan Nagy, handsome, well-mannered, enthusiastic, with sturdy partnering arms. Because of my stuttering English and the necessity of using an interpreter, the rehearsals were endless and tiresome. Ivan demonstrated prodigies of alertness and thoughtfulness. From the first rehearsal an atmosphere of friendliness arose

Rehearsing GISELLE *with Erik Bruhn*

that cemented itself with the years. I soon began to relate to him as if he were a brother. He patiently tolerated the whims I tend to inflict on those close to me. When I get upset or annoyed by something, I pour out my feelings at my friends, who unwillingly become my scapegoats—a rather peculiar bonus they receive along with my genuine attachment and affection toward them. Ivan understood me very soon and was tolerant and indulgent with all my emotionalism. Because I could not express myself properly in English, sometimes my requests to Ivan sounded like orders and seemed to be rude, or even ridiculous. He always displayed incredible tact and did not raise an eyebrow when I demanded, "Ivan, put me on your soldier."

His gallantry was a moral support to me throughout this first *Giselle*, during which I felt so ill at ease. Through tremendous strain and tension, I somehow mastered the technical aspects of the performance. Feeling elated after the successfully performed variation in Act I, I went limp during a curtsy and fell to the side in front of the public. In Russia such things are not given any importance—they have nothing to do with artistry—but here the critics saw in it a very serious fault, damaging the performance.

My partnership with Erik took place at a later date. I danced the full *Giselle* with him, but more frequently the pas de deux from Act II, as well as *Les Sylphides, La Sylphide, The River, The Miraculous Mandarin,* and John Neumeier's *Epilogue.* Most of all I appreciate Erik's unique combination of innate aristocratic manners with technical virtuosity, his rare sensibility as an actor, and his sense of atmosphere on stage. We immediately established psychological contact, since I quickly respond to the noble and refined qualities of such an artist. Unfortunately, I danced with him as his artistic career was declining. Had we met earlier, I am sure a long and most harmonious partnership would have evolved. I still love his presence at rehearsals and value his comments, which are always in good taste and to the point.

Epilogue was my first experience in neo-classical style in the West. Neumeier's choreography seemed to me rather exciting, and the movements had real emotional depth. I regarded *Epilogue* as an existential ballet about two lonely human beings who long for each other and desperately try to understand each other, while something prevents them from achieving the closeness they desire. The choreography is based on a tremendous inner tension; before starting to dance, one has to feel enormous energy in the muscles, set them going, but still hold back. But emotional restraint does not come easily to me, and I had to master this particular skill.

And Neumeier's choreography is not the only one that requires this restraint; it often seemed to me that the main feature of Western dancing was its subdued emotional content. *Epilogue* somehow changed my general approach to ballet expressiveness. Since my early days in the Kirov, I had believed that the more I poured out my emotional resources on stage, the more desirable the result. Now I realized that I didn't have to use all my energy on stage to achieve tremendous expressiveness. The experience with *Epilogue* helped me learn to regulate my energy properly in *Giselle* and *Swan Lake,* and they went more successfully after I had managed to adjust my emotional means to my artistic needs.

Working on the pas de deux from *The River* brought me another discovery: the jazz of Duke Ellington. In the beginning Erik and I floundered in this River rather desperately. Both of us felt awkward; we couldn't catch the rhythm and the right timing. I had never dealt with jazz before and although I had been somewhat familiar with it since my childhood—my stepfather and stepbrother still play it—its beat does not run in my blood.

While rehearsing with Alvin Ailey I realized how strongly a classically trained body differs from that of a jazz dancer. Jazz demands an immediate reaction of the muscles to the beat and an absolute freedom not given to classical dancers. Classical dancing is an embroidering on a given canvas; our bodies are equipped with some physical capabilities owing to which they are able to execute certain combinations of steps. We are taught to obey choreographic patterns and adjust our physical abilities and dance experience to them, and before starting to perform movements, we give appropriate tasks to the various parts of our body. Classical dancers are not able to get rid at once of that hard-won permanent control over their bodies and acquire instead a muscularly unpredictable response to a jazz beat. My daily training strictly insists where this leg will go, or that arm; it excludes free plasticity. Our freedom in ballet lies essentially in our ability to express ourselves in terms of ballet patterns, in the liberation of inner feelings but not of the body itself, in that balance between our body, obedient to choreographic patterns, and its hidden spirit, whose instrument our body essentially is. To liberate my body from my classical heritage just for a short while and to achieve a spontaneity of muscular reactions to jazz became an obsession. I desperately attempted to realize the concentrations of jazz dancing as opposed to those of classical dancing: in the latter our concentration, as I say, covers the whole body—our legs, arms, the positioning of the head—and excludes any improvisations, whereas jazz demands quite the opposite.

I was amazed at the remarkable way the Puerto Ricans or Brazilians moved; jazz for them, its beat and rhythm, are like Slavic lyrical melodies for Russians. A few years later I watched children dancing jazz in Rio de Janeiro and almost died from envy—they possessed a spontaneous sense of rhythm and an abandon I could only dream of.

Erik and I went to a Puerto Rican discotheque to learn the feeling of jazz. Of course, I did not dare show up on the dance floor—I merely watched—but some sense of syncopated beat did come to me, and I managed to keep it until the premiere. Afterward, a critic wrote that I danced jazz as if I had been doing it all my life, which sounded flattering. Alas, my jazz experience evaporated as quickly as it came to me. If I had to dance jazz again, I would rush to a discotheque to recharge my batteries.

Coppélia and *La Fille Mal Gardée* were also totally new for me. Both were comic ballets, and this in itself was enough to interest me, in spite of their rather trivial choreography. In Russia I had danced a comic part only once, in *Cinderella;* in the West the roles of Swanilda and Lise gave me a new opportunity to try my comedy skills. (I still don't know if I really have a gift for comedy or just an ability to improvise on the stage. In England they do not know this side of my dance personality.)

The two ballets are similar in that they don't have a firm choreographic construction, and the "holes" in their structure have to be filled by each individual dancer's improvisations. Therefore, in both ballets I was happily improvising, and I feel a real satisfaction when my spontaneous finds hit the target. But it is very difficult to improvise in such amorphous ballets: the choreography in no way helps you find the appropriate mood for your improvising. The combinations of steps are rather bland, they carry no characterization of the role—they don't suggest any character features. In some way, *Coppélia* is even more difficult for me than *Giselle,* though it is hard to compare the two roles from the point of view of physical strain. *Coppélia* is one continuous dance that lacks any specific style (in contrast to the romantic tone of *Giselle*), and performing its innumerable eccentric tricks on the stage consumes a lot of energy. Unfortunately, whatever improvisations you come up with do not improve the essential choreographic pattern of *Coppélia:* they are restricted by its framework.

Probably, in Ashton's *La Fille Mal Gardée* I could not have slackened the reins and frolicked around as much as I did at ABT: Ashton's logical and strict choreographic structure demands a complete obedience. And yet, it might be easier to find fresh colors and even comic nuances in it: the choreography would help me find the necessary state of mind, and I wouldn't feel abandoned to my own intuition; I wouldn't have to "self-ignite."

While the choreography of the two ballets at ABT was equally faceless, it was easier for me to perform *Fille* (I mean only the acting, not the physical strain), because it is nearer to a farce or to the genre termed "vaudeville" in Russia, a comedy of situations with dances and songs. If any comic trick looks appropriate, it helps the overall comedy. Lise is a more childlike character than Swanilda, who already has a budding womanhood in her. Lise is just a mischievous, cunning girl, and this was my clue for the role: I played it in the pure vaudeville style.

Coppélia does not belong to any definite genre. An amorphous comedy vaguely related to Hoffmann's story, it reveals a certain irony toward the

Top: Curtain call for LES SYLPHIDES
—first performance with Erik Bruhn

Bottom: LA SYLPHIDE *rehearsal*

beginning Industrial Revolution in Europe. In the story the increasing mechanistic nature of life is defeated, and a real human being triumphs over a puppet (the robot of the future). In the ballet version of *Coppélia*, the character of Swanilda is the incarnation of a woman's inventive enterprise. I decided to make my Swanilda more individual, to give her temperament and stamina. I wanted to move the whole ballet toward farce by my use of improvisation. Otherwise the whole performance looks like a set of nice clichés from an assortment of other ballets, while the plot makes one think of a sugary story from a book for children of good families. I still like one of my spontaneous finds that came upon me as suddenly as when many years ago my Affected Sister from *Cinderella* started compulsively chewing her own shoe, unable to cope with her helpless despair. In the wedding scene my Swanilda feverishly started to eat . . . the flowers. I liked the grotesque coloring, and I had the impression that the public liked it too, even if the critics didn't accept it: they saw it as an unnecessary exaggeration. But I still believe that liberties like this one give spice and freshness to the clichés of *Coppélia*.

As for *La Sylphide*, I at once felt natural in Bournonville's style, and had no particular difficulties, after the training I had received at the Vaganova School that combined the French, the Italian, and the Russian traditions, and after my long years of friendship with the romantic ballet and the experience of *Giselle* and *Les Sylphides*.

I rehearsed my role with Erik Bruhn, whose version is slightly different from the original Danish version that I learned later from Flemming Flindt. Erik slightly adapted the style of Bournonville to modern tastes; he skipped a part of the obsolete pantomime and staged the approaches to jetés not after Bournonville but closer to *Giselle* and late romantic tradition. The problem was that Bournonville choreographed his ballets for a small stage. From this comes his precision in elaborating the small-scale technique, attitudes, and innumerable brisés. It also influenced the specific of his jeté, which is high but without a real soaring; it is performed on the spot, without a preparation, so it is always hard to jump up high. It looks like floating in the air, without traversing a real space. Bournonville had a "short-range" design; the "long-range" construction appears only in Petipa's work staged for the spacious Maryinsky stage. I felt uncomfortable doing the original jetés designed by Bournonville, while Erik allowed me to push myself into a jeté as I had always done in *Giselle*.

There also was another problem, purely stylistic. The romantic style of *La Sylphide* differs from that of *Giselle:* it is more naïve and archaic, therefore it demands a more elaborate performance, with its own aesthetic overtones. The naïve manner of *La Sylphide,* dominated by light flying movements, reflects a specific mood of playful joy and warm femininity emanating from the ethereal image of the Sylphide.

The romantic ideal of eternal femininity is focused in her differently than in Giselle: she is the symbol of feminine inconstancy and coquetry, she is the pure light charm of femininity, even if she is not flesh and blood. And though she is incorporeal, she has nothing of the "world beyond our world" so characteristic of the mysterious second act of *Giselle*. The charm of the second act of *La Sylphide* is in its warm colors, in its near-pastel impressionism, when the Sylphide is playing in the wood with her friends, tempting and teasing James.

La Sylphide also has an element of the romantic drama, but it is much lighter than in *Giselle:* it is a fairy tale that cannot be made too tragic. The heroine knows that she cannot enjoy carnal love and sensual intimacy with a man, but she is irresistibly attracted to him, as if testing her charm. There is a peculiar excitement in her movements when she touches James slightly and then flies away, like a butterfly circling a fire that may at any moment burn her wings.

To grasp this elusive lightness of the Sylphide, I did what I had done years earlier, when I was working on *Giselle* — I looked again and again through the lithographs of Taglioni and Grisi, slightly coloring my movements to imitate the romantic "olden days." I tried to convey the easy changes in her mood, from sadness to joy, from light playfulness to elegiac reflection. It was a part of my acting task. The most difficult moment was in the first act, when she is sad and turns away from the audience; this change of mood must be expressed, literally, by the dancer's back.

Since my debut in *La Sylphide,* each performance of this enchanting ballet reinforces my experience in its romantic pastel vocabulary that from the beginning came to me so much more easily than the language of Tudor's ballets, which I was also tackling for the first time.

I was ecstatic about Tudor's ballets while still in London, but when I met him their creator impressed me even more. I already was aware that at ABT he was unusually respected and feared, and I was somewhat nervous when I saw him for the first time: tall, lean, with a flat and almost bald head, he reminded me for a moment of the figure of an inquisitor. His eyes especially made a deep impression on me: transparent, bottomless, impenetrable. There was about him that special air of English reserve which to the Russian eye seems almost like coldness. But all of that disappeared when he began to move, to act out his ballets at rehearsal. In the movements of his hands, his thin fingers, his neck, in his carriage, there was such internal animation and logic that it was impossible for me not to catch fire, not to absorb this into myself. Moreover, there was one thing which drew me to him — his sense of humor of an especially caustic nature. At rehearsals he was not sparing of sarcastic remarks, sometimes bringing the dancers of ABT to the point of tears.

By nature I react well to criticism, since the main thing for me is to grasp the essence of critical remarks. Moreover, someone caustic is a special sort of challenge for me; I immediately experience a desire to parry, to involve myself in what is called the battle of wits. At the beginning, owing to the poverty of my English, many of Tudor's cutting remarks passed me by; subsequently, in the heat and tension of the moment, I would suddenly acquire my own sharpness of language. I would start to defend myself and to fight back, to the absolute horror of my colleagues, who would themselves simply freeze before Tudor. He would answer me in kind, and the inequality of ability in these linguistic duels only made them more heated. In a word, emotional contact sprang up between us, and soon it turned into friendship.

Many things about him as a person intrigued me, beginning with his Zen Buddhism. When I found out that he got up at five in the morning in order to be on the roof at six for meditation, I decided to get up on his roof before dawn with him, to see how he went about it. Unfortunately (or fortunately) my alarm clock let me down and my plan remained unrealized.

Our rehearsals together were easy and relaxed in spite of our sharp altercations; he would sometimes make me burst out laughing and I would feel purged inside, free of the tension that accompanied my first two years in America. I recall a rehearsal for *Romeo and Juliet* in which he showed me how Juliet covers her eyes from the blinding rays of the morning sun which signal her parting from her beloved. "Imagine that you've caught sight of Stalin or Hitler and cover your face in terror," he joked. And I immediately achieved the necessary state. But more frequently he did not wish to help me in this way; he enjoyed my helplessness, tossing me like a puppy into the flow of his ballets, then observing whether I could swim or not. At rehearsals, he was not so much sparing as he was stingy with his encouragement and commentary. When I was working on his *Dark Elegies,* I simply forgot that I was dancing a village girl, just overlooked it! It never occurred to Tudor to remind me, though he realized that I had chosen a quite inappropriate manner. He was silent, as if testing me, waiting to see how I would extricate myself. Fortunately, one of my colleagues mentioned my "social status" to me almost on the eve of the premiere, and I did not fall into Tudor's trap.

People in the troupe were amazed at how quickly I was able to assimilate this new style. From the point of view of balletic vocabulary, Tudor's choreographic language was not impossibly new or difficult for me, especially after Yakobson's ballets. The difficulty and newness of his choreography resided in something else—its emotional fullness, its manner of expressing feeling which is so essentially different between the Russians and the English. In Russia, I was not accustomed to hobble my feelings on the stage in any way, only to control them and to dance them with profuse abundance. Russians are not ashamed of emotional openness, and in this sense they are much less children of civilization, less dependent on civilization's laws, than the English. In Tudor's ballets, the heroine—whether she be Hagar in *Pillar of Fire* or Caroline in *Lilac Garden*—is consumed by her passion, her turbulent feelings, but the form of expression is extremely restrained, and not very Russian. I had to redirect my emotions into another channel, to restrain myself, to be as expressive as possible with limited gestures, to be "a flame under ice," to use Stendhal's expression. And achieving this new expressiveness took tremendous effort.

Tudor felt that the atmosphere of his ballets was Chekhovian, but unfortunately I did not see this in them. The difference in our cultural experience was making itself felt. The similarity seemed superficial to me; it is true that, as with Chekhov, most of Tudor's characters are provincials, little people in small towns, tortured by their passions. But I did not sense in them the main thing that makes a Chekhovian character unique: the longing for a new life in which there will be a spiritual center, a high goal—whether service to others or creative work—without which existence is rendered meaningless. For instance, I felt nothing of the kind in Hagar—an embittered old maid, desperate from her inability to find a man. . . . It seemed to me that this exhausted her character, so dissimilar to mine! I was quite unable to get into the skin of this ill-fated spinster, or rather to feel her with my own skin.

The premiere of *Pillar of Fire* did not bring me any internal satisfaction. I did not feel natural in the role in a way that would have prevented my movements from being empty and formal. And although others seemed pleased after my performance, I sat in my dressing room, trembling, as I waited for Tudor. I feared his opinion more than anything. What would he say? Finally he appeared, sat down on a chair, and remained silent for a long time. At last he said: "How come you were always heading for the house? Well, okay, despair, you were trapped, but why head for the house?" I hadn't actually noticed that, feeling instinctively uncomfortable on stage, I was constantly straining toward the house, as if it were a refuge. Tudor said nothing else and left. This was exactly like him.

I danced three more performances and nothing seemed right, though apparently Tudor and the public were satisfied. But I knew that my Hagar was inadequate. At this point, strangely enough, Chekhov came to my aid, or rather the Soviet film of his *Lady with the Dog*, which Tudor liked very much. It was not even the film itself which helped but the sublime expression which Savina, who played the lead, conveyed with her clear eyes, longing for love while disbelieving in it, and nonetheless expecting internal renewal from it. I simply felt the expression of those eyes physically, and everything fell into place. And after the next performance, Tudor said to me: "Now, you're doing what you have to."

I liked dancing his *Romeo and Juliet* very much, although after every performance I had a strange feeling, as though I had been given an opportunity to express myself and was constantly on the verge of opening my mouth—but no sound would come, no matter how much I strained. Tudor's choreography was too tight for me, too illustrative, and his compositions reminded me of an animated tapestry in the manner of the Pre-Raphaelites. Meanwhile, I wanted to dance the Juliet of Shakespeare, of whom there is not the slightest notion in the music of Delius—moderately aesthetic, moderately recherché, pleasant to the ear. Tudor's illustrative or decorative approach—call it what you will—corresponds closely to the spirit of Delius's music, but it did not strike any deeper spiritual notes in me, just as the paintings of the Pre-Raphaelites leave me cold.

The more I worked with Tudor, the more I became aware of one of his peculiarities: he did not like to prepare roles carefully, but left to the dancer the freedom to improvise and express himself, whereas at that time what I needed was a good bridle. Rehearsing the extremely compressed lines of *Lilac Garden* and simultaneously working on other ballets, I found myself in a very difficult situation. I realized that not only had I failed in getting used to the subtle Proustian atmosphere of the ballet, I had not even been able to learn my entrances and the sequence of the work. Memory eluded me—my head was exploding with the abundance of information squeezed into it. I panicked and phoned Tudor to ask him to come to my apartment and note down my entrances to the music. The Inquisitor took pity on his victim and appeared before me with his crooked little smile. He understood my agitation and seemed actually touched by my nervousness over the debut. At the same time, he took obvious pleasure in my helplessness. This rehearsal of *Lilac Garden* to the music, at home, gave me much more than the regular rehearsals; every word of Tudor's hit the mark immediately. And in those three hours or so I learned more about my Caroline than I had dreamed of during the entire rehearsal time (infernally short). Nonetheless, I still was not sure of the sequence and, more important, still got mixed up in the musical cues.

"Will you keep watch over me from the wings, Antony?" I asked.

"Ha, ha!" he responded. "Don't expect that. I'll get my pleasure out of this spectacle in the audience."

I can imagine how many slips I made in my first performance of *Lilac Garden*, but Tudor seemed satisfied, although I never really knew whether he liked my work or not. But later, bringing in a new performer for the ballet, he asked me to show her Caroline and kept saying, "Watch how she moves—that's the way to do it."

In *Lilac Garden* as much as in *Pillar* I suffered from the starkness of the choreographic material, because my expressive nature rebelled against Tudor's restraint. My Russian training was coming through, plus my individual expressivity, which Yakobson had developed and encouraged in me. My muscles could not control themselves, my body strained toward a completely unshackled expression disruptive to the Tudor style. On the other hand, for his dance vocabulary I lacked that understatement through which my movements might have extended themselves and achieved a new dimension. Therefore, for all my love of the subtle and poetic atmosphere of *Lilac Garden,* I never came to terms with the ballet and probably never danced it to the best of my abilities.

During my first years in America, one of the most interesting ballets I danced was Balanchine's *Apollo.* Unfortunately it was soon dropped from ABT's repertoire. This is one of my favorite Balanchine ballets, along with *Prodigal Son, Concerto Barocco, Symphony in C,* and *The Four Temperaments*—all of which I dream of dancing someday.

At that time, I was not entirely ready to cope with Balanchine's style technically, since I had not yet completely mastered the academic style of Petipa from which Balanchine had grown as a choreographer. His combinations are built on those elements of the classical dance which are studied daily in the classroom. But the noteworthy feature of Balanchine's style makes itself felt in the extreme density of the movements, performed in the unit of time with very swift tempo. Only specially trained dancers are able to deal with Balanchine's rapid tempo and style, because it demands physical endurance and a special ability of the body to move at very high speed. The velocity of this particular style indirectly reflects the tendency of our century, as manifested in its space flights, the tremendous speed of its jet planes. I feel in it the accelerated tempo of our life, its nervous and syncopated throbbing.

This staccato style does not come to Russian dancers easily, because our approach to performing movements is quite different. We are taught to feel our muscles by executing steps that seem to be passing through our whole body, and after being felt they demand to be emotionally expressed by the body through pure classical means. Least of all are we apt to dance mechanically, whereas Balanchine's style is based on a mechanical technique whose virtuoso combinations are given to the body as its main task to undertake and perform. Thus Balanchine's style pursues the pure relationship between technique and music; technique is used for the beauty of technique per se.

Apollo, for me, was a kind of introduction to Balanchine's aesthetics. I know few contemporary ballets in which the music and the choreography are so naturally knitted together into a single whole; sometimes you cannot tell which gives rise to which. In *Apollo,* one of Balanchine's early ballets, he had not entirely cut the umbilical cord with a traditional ballet plot; thus it tends toward an abstraction that is presented in its essentially neoclassical form. The movements and emotions in *Apollo* seem crystallized, as if they had passed through some creative distillation. The elements of choreography are basically simple and do not demand any task of interpreting—they just have to be performed properly. The beauty of *Apollo*'s choreography lies in the strict correspondence of these crystallized elements to the music, in their absolute harmony. And so my goal was to achieve this purity in performing each element, no matter how simple it might be. The sense of absolutely perfect choreography to which I attempted to subjugate my abilities provided very special satisfaction that never left me during the rehearsals and performances. The only hitch was that the syncopated coda did not come to me instantly. My inexperience in dancing to jazz rhythms took a lot of energy to cope with. But at the first performance it came out quite decently.

Theme and Variations revealed itself to be very complicated. I rehearsed it with Balanchine himself. This was at ABT, where he had not shown up for years. After the rehearsal I asked him for his reactions but he seemed to be satisfied with me, merely commenting that I wasn't able to spot during pirouettes (this had always been a weak point with me). In other words, I wasn't able to turn my head faster than my body. It's understandable: at that time my technique was still essentially romantic, which led my body to execute steps in a cantilena-like manner without any disconnection in the movements of my arms and legs. Balanchine's combinations in *Theme* are very often based on a staccato-like disconnection, with arms, legs, and head seeming to pursue different tasks depending on which one is to achieve the desired syncopating effect. (My "slowness upstairs" was apparent in performance: doing fast rotations in the first variation, I could not get my bearings for a moment and tended to keep my whole body under control as I used to, whereas one ought merely to control its different parts moving in disunity. My head would be spinning and I would be close to fainting.)

Nevertheless, everything went rather smoothly at rehearsal, and my sense of security never left me. Alas, it evaporated during performance, seriously affecting my dancing. For me this sense of security is, in a way, a pledge of success: when I am sure of myself on stage, I instantly catch the given rhythm that makes my body move properly. The situation with *Theme* was complicated, since Balanchine's plotless choreography did not motivate my inner life. In other words, from the outset the body was to be put into the choreographic frame and rely only upon its own endurance and the appropriate physical reactions. A ballerina trained mostly in the classical story-ballet of Petipa has a hard time switching immediately, since her body expects to be guided by the logic of plot at least.

In *Theme* I felt totally on my own, without any support. At rehearsals I watched myself in mirrors that mercilessly reflected all my mistakes, even the tiniest slips. That was my "correcting eye" and my guide. I oriented myself according to the prompting of the mirror. But in order to dance *Theme* in actual performance, I had to do without my guide—I had to feel that "correcting eye" inside me, providing and enhancing my security.

This security is really freedom from any external control: it assumes the

Top left: APOLLO, *with Ivan Nagy*

Top right: Rehearsing DON QUIXOTE *with Ivan Nagy*

Bottom right: APOLLO *rehearsal*

body's total subordination to inner control. Because I lacked experience with Balanchine's style, I felt pretty helpless during performance. And dancing *Theme* at the Kennedy Center in Washington, I was quite simply inadequate. In the first variation I wasn't able to maintain the mechanical repetition of one and the same combination—pas de chat, soutenu, double pirouette from fifth position—and I could manage only one sequence. I ought to have been working with the uniformity of a metronome, distributing my energy equally for each combination. Otherwise it is easy to get the body off-center. And that was what happened to me. I was accustomed to spending my energy too spontaneously; I "poured myself out" in the first combination and couldn't attack the second one physically. I should have continued working on *Theme,* as I had done with Odile, but the schedule of performances was so strenuous that, at the time, I had no chance to master the mechanics of the Balanchine style. And I reserve the right to return to *Theme* now that I have better stamina and my feet are much more used to demands like these.

For me, Balanchine is a genius, because he alone in the twentieth century has created a unique style and a choreographic lexicon, the richness and inventiveness of which never fail to astonish. Also, he does not age with the years—his early ballets (my favorites) are much more contemporary than many of today's ultra-modern works by other choreographers. I never cease to be enchanted by Balanchine's taste and by that choreographic musicality he possesses as no one else does.

Balanchine calls himself a student of Petipa, and he is the only person in the ballet world who has gone beyond Petipa. Balanchine used the old principle of classical ballet—"beauty in the geometry of movement and the geometry of beauty"—with contemporary perception. He brought the classical ballet to America and built an audience for it here. More, he created his own ballet culture, and it became part of American culture in the twentieth century. He joined the traditions of the Russian ballet, which had been refined by the Diaghilev seasons abroad and taken over by Europe, with the American theatrical tradition. And only an experienced balletic eye can evaluate the tact and the taste with which he achieved this transplanting of a European art in soil unfamiliar to him.

He is a most skilled gardener. The tree he planted has bloomed magnificently: it took root and grew and produced such a luxuriant crown. Petipa had once been inspired by Offenbachian innovations during his Parisian seasons, then introduced the pas emboîté, later directly associated with the cancan of the Toulouse-Lautrec epoch. In the same way, Balanchine filled out the old classical vocabulary with new movements—taken even from the music hall and popular American shows—to which he gave his own contribution on Broadway, and he reconstituted the combinations, creating an entirely new choreographic lexicon.

Probably the American approach in using music for dancing on Broadway somehow stimulated the creation of the new Balanchine aesthetics. Dancing became not a vehicle for expressing some plot or conveying a certain message; its emotional impact was dictated by dance in itself, and it did not pursue any informative tasks whatsoever. No wonder Balanchine was fascinated by the artistry of Fred Astaire on the screen, who like no one else in America turned dancing into the direct demonstration of an astonishing musicality, a sense of rhythm, and a muscular knack, performing the most intricate tricks.

Balanchine is also unique in having managed to develop a company of classical dancers out of Americans devoid of the traditions of Russian training. In fact the lack of that classical professionalism (whose level, incidentally, was not that high even in the Diaghilev company—Balanchine was upset by this just at the beginning of his career in the West) became a kind of creative stimulant for Balanchine. He created his *Serenade* in the wake of Fokine simply to teach his young dancers certain little lessons and "make a ballet that wouldn't show how badly they danced"—his own words. But later on, this process of adjusting classical technique to the abilities of American performers and to the underdeveloped taste of the local ballet audience led to his search for new balletic expressiveness beyond Petipa's classical vocabulary or Fokine's legacy.

When Balanchine came back to Russia for the first time to present his ballets in the former Maryinsky—still the same blue velvet and gilded hall—he was met with enthusiasm by the rather conservative and quite demanding Leningrad audience. I recall how many knowledgeable people said, "Balanchine has brought us our future, which was not permitted to come to fruition in Russia." I take the liberty of not entirely agreeing.

The Russian ballet, to which George Balanchine is organically tied, has always been famous for the directness of its lyric communication with the audience. The spirit of a Pavlova, a Ulanova, became the incarnation of this communication. This spirit of humanity created a bridge between the Russian ballet—functioning in the abstract language of the classical dance—and life itself. Geometry breathed emotionality; it was spiritualized in this way, as if overcoming or even brushing aside its abstractness.

Balanchine turned the ballet sharply in the direction of plotlessness that can be perceived as abstraction. And in this I see a sign of the aesthetics of our "head-oriented" age. As I view it, with Balanchine, ballet vocabulary became not only an expression of the music's style, but an analogue or parallel created in the language of another art—the language of dance. By rejecting pantomime and other ways of illustrating the meaning of dance (ways which Fokine, for instance, fought for), Balanchine put ballet on the level of structural density that is generally peculiar to music, density bordering on abstraction. Indeed, when we listen to music, a specific plastic image does not arise; it is the choreographic design and the dancer's body which make music concrete. Balanchine's aesthetics, essentially formal, are built on an overcoming of the concrete body. In *Symphony in C, Concerto Barocco,* or *Stravinsky Violin Concerto* (I take Balanchine masterworks later than *Prodigal Son* or *Apollo*), he tries to create, insofar as possible, an intricate choreographic order containing within itself a range of meanings. The spectator, aside from purely enjoying the beauty and musicality of composition, is invited to find and define these meanings for himself. In this, I think there is a certain subtle intellectual pleasure, which is why, one assumes, intellectuals of all varieties are so drawn to Balanchine.

It is quite understandable why Balanchine, unlike Petipa, in whose time there was very little good music for ballet, has rarely worked with bad composers. And not by accident. Each—Stravinsky, Mozart, Gluck, Ravel, Tchaikovsky, Bizet, Hindemith—provides him with a level and density of musical texture that can be expressed in the dance only by the sensitive and refined language he handles so skillfully. In Balanchine's ballets the dancers form an orchestra of musical instruments that he alone can play. His company is a one-choreographer-ballet theatre (apart from the large contribution by Jerome Robbins), where everyone must strictly follow the clue he has given. It is quite natural that he dislikes—or, to put it more exactly, has avoided—real "stars." Balanchine needs only obedient performers, whereas stars regard themselves not as mere performers but as active participants in the creative process. I must add that Russian stars are particularly difficult in this respect, because the Russian tradition at its best—exemplified by Chabukiani, Ulanova, Plisetskaya, Nureyev—has always implied a close creative collaboration between the choreographer and the dancer. Balanchine has not until now accepted such individual talents: in his system of abstract ballet they would be out of place, because they must be the first among equals, like the first violin playing a solo in an orchestra conducted by him. He is the conductor, the choreographer, the creator, the demiurge.

I had a difficult time working as an anonymous element in his system because from my very first exercises in dance class, I was taught to express myself in a dance, to infuse it with my own feelings, to transform it into a spiritual phenomenon. And my individual performing style is different—my body sings dancing in a very cantilena-like way. The prevailing style of Balanchine, with its choreographic intensity in time, is closer to fast speech than to singing.

The style of Balanchine is sometimes called impersonal: a dancer must dissolve his individuality in the style of the maestro. He must never be conspicuous, like a striking detail in a picture—he must be a part of the whole. Of course, in reality it doesn't happen that way. Remarkable dancers from Balanchine's company such as Edward Villella, Violette Verdy, Allegra Kent, and Arthur Mitchell, who came to Russia in 1962, impressed us so much because their individual gifts combined so well with Balan-chine's style. (No doubt this is what will happen with Baryshnikov.) That is why when I worked on Balanchine's ballets, my primary problem was one of style: I had to find a way to submit my artistic possibilities to his creative principles, to make his principles mine, while in ballets without those sto-ries which can be so helpful in prompting the necessary state of mind.

Balanchine's art, like a prism, brought together the main trends of our twentieth century; and so his desire to find a harmony in discordance, his mistrust of any message implying a didactic purpose, his escape into the realm of pure, disinterested beauty alien to those ideological notions so compromised in our time. But I personally cannot accept this escape into "pure beauty," with its music and faultless inner construction as the defini-tive attitude to reality, as an aesthetic credo. The imperfections of real life, its conflicts, human dramas, and emotions still move me, and I want to tell about them in the language of dance. That is why I prefer ballets in which there is room for an interpretation, where I can partially express my own human experience, in the hope it will find a response in someone's heart. In my hierarchy of art, emotional values are placed much higher than abstract or formal ones. I am sure they will live as long as human life con-tinues, as long as people have sympathy and compassion for one another and need art to draw their energy from.

From my first days at ABT, my life assumed such a crazy pace that now I wonder how I managed to survive. As if trying to justify my flight from Russia, I got parts in so many ballets, all at once, that I found myself on a superhuman schedule: for the 1971–72 season I was learning a number of roles at one time, rehearsing eight hours a day, and then dancing at night on stage. (All this after the Kirov, where at most I danced three or four performances a month, first working out every detail of a role with my nu-merous teachers and tutors, and where to speak of a rehearsal on the same day as a performance would have been blasphemy. This had been the case since the days of Kschessinskaya and Karsavina at least. On the day of a performance we were supposed to have a good rest, to accumulate the energy that was later to be poured out before the audience.) In comparison to the Kirov vacation resort, ABT was drudgery. I was falling off my feet after the endless rehearsals, performances, and innumerable interviews I was giving at that time, sometimes several a day.

Probably this immense strain in its own strange way freed me of many of the psychological problems often confronted by emigrants. I had only one preoccupation: not to lose what I had learned during the day's rehearsals. Never before had I lived so intensely—I was working myself to death. And never before had I danced so badly from a technical point of view. I felt sure of myself only in romantic technique, but the variety of styles I met with at ABT demanded a large variety of techniques, and at that time I did not have the ability to switch over immediately from one style to another. I saw that leading dancers at ABT passed easily from classic to neo-classic or modern ballets without deep insight into the subtleties of their respective styles. Technically they could perform any combination of movements; they cared more than anything else about the spectacular effect of their performances. Their purely rational approach to movement was highly economical in comparison with the Russian school, as their dancing was based only on a necessary set of technical skills that guaranteed the needed theatrical effect. In other words, the guiding principle of the Russian school, by which a dancer must sense a movement with his entire body, was foreign to them; for them a movement was just a mechanical task assigned to their bodies. My Russian background made me aware of many shortcomings in their approach: they neglected the plié that makes a dancer's legs particularly expressive, that makes legs almost as eloquent as arms; they did not have sufficient port de bras and épaulement, therefore losing the expressivity of the shoulders and the chest. They were much less generous in emotions than Russian dancers are, and in their movements I did not feel the abandon that makes it possible to "transcend" the movement, to step out into a new dimension. For them every style consisted only of a certain set of movements there to be coped with, not unlike a challenge in sports. I do not mean to say that they lacked artistry, but their art depended more on their personal charm and temperament, and their artistic achievements were based rather on exploiting the plastic possibilities of their bodies than on actually using them. Like athletes, they were after spectacular effects that utilized only the external resources of the body, ignoring its inner potential.

For me, on the contrary, each individual style meant a specific sense of movement, a specific working of the muscles: I could not use my arms identically in *Giselle* and in *Swan Lake,* or perform arabesques exactly the same way in every ballet. During this period, for the first time, I started pondering over the expressive means the Kirov had armed me with for the new life I had chosen. I started looking for a way to adapt my Russian training to the interpretation of the numerous roles I faced in ABT's wide repertoire. The answer did not come at once; the process of self-realization spanned several years of intense work. Only now do I clearly understand the lessons of the Kirov and the inheritance it gave me.

A dancer's life is a slow process of understanding one's own body, its plastic possibilities and limitations. In Russia I never really thought about all this; I was surrounded by many teachers and nurses who seemed to know everything, so I didn't need to. They all followed the Vaganova method, which presupposed a common aesthetic, common values and choices, that I automatically shared with them. I had a total faith in my tutors and could grow quietly under their vigilant supervision.

The strength of the Kirov Ballet, the polished brilliance of its romantic and classical styles, stemmed from a strict determination of each dancer's physique, appearance, and technical resources. The Kirov maintained a hierarchy of genres born in the times of Didelot and Petipa, when all dancers were strictly classified into danseurs nobles, romantic ballerinas, classical ballerinas, ingenues, or "demi-caractère." Such concentration along one line encouraged the development of individual talents: Alla Osipenko, a ballerina of classical line and training, would not be put into a romantic ballet, and Valery Panov would not get a danseur noble role. Of course, there were dancers like Alla Shelest or Dudinskaya whose repertoire included virtually all the classical roles, owing to their vast dance amplitude, but even so each of them had a favorite sphere of her own. Each of us knew the domain that was hers, each of us developed the specific technical and acting skills necessary for her particular line, and, as a result, each of us had a strongly developed sense of personal style.

For me a ballet without a sense of style is a ballet that cannot provoke empathy; it is just a sequence of movements, even when their execution is very spectacular. But it is hard to define what I mean by a sense of style. Maybe it is the knowledge of what must *not* be done in a romantic or a classical ballet. In both cases it is a particular system of restrictions concerning the positions of arms, hands, feet, chest, shoulders, and head. If we stop observing these restrictions, all ballets will look alike, and the variety of aesthetic impressions will be lost. The spectators will lose more than anyone else, even those who are not experts in stylistic subtleties, for if they are only seeing dancers who approach ballet as a sport, they will never know the difference between the plastic beauty of *Giselle* and that of *Sleeping Beauty*, merely the difference between their stories.

This sense of style I brought from the Kirov. Here are the roots of my oversensitivity to small details and my organic inability to "cheat" on the stage. When I dance *Swan Lake*, I try to make every finger "talk," and I know there are no limits to perfecting one's expressive means. Any other way of dancing is inconceivable to me.

I cannot create the illusory impression of ease in my performance when there is no ease in my legs, in my whole body. I cannot cheat by changing the choreography slightly to make it easier for myself, just as I am unable to conceal the absence of technique behind acting tricks or by distorting my physical nature. The Kirov taught me a constant self-criticism, which, combined with my innate perfectionism, made my first years in the West very difficult psychologically. The difficulties also came from a different source. A performer's fixed line in the Kirov was the foundation for the highest artistic development *along this line*, but it could also turn into a serious obstacle for those whose inner resources exceeded the limits of this line. I was one of the few who belonged to the latter category, and the roots of my conflict with the Kirov lay precisely in this imposed limitation. My spiritual development was very intense and grew much faster than my repertoire. This suppressed passion strove to emerge, yet outside my romantic roles, it

found an outlet only in Yakobson's neo-classical ballets. The elasticity his demands gave to my muscles, the coordination and general relaxation I had learned working on his ballets, was immensely helpful to me in approaching the choreographies of Antony Tudor, Glen Tetley, and Jerome Robbins. Many dancers of the Kirov Company were content with the limitations imposed on them; for instance, Kolpakova was happy with what she had and probably even today dances Giselle or Aurora with the same enthusiasm. Those limitations in the Kirov are more rigid now than they were in the old Maryinsky. Anna Pavlova used to dance Kitry and the Sleeping Beauty and even Mercedes in *Don Quixote*, whereas they never let me dance in *Don Quixote*, believing that Kitry was a soubrette, not a romantic part; and I was given Aurora very late, and only for a tour in Japan.

All this is why the variety of the ABT repertoire fell on me like an unbearable burden: even technically I was not prepared to cope with it. I was saved by something that I fully recognized only in the West: despite my classical line and shape, I have a neo-classical "nucleus." My body depends on my state of mind and is influenced by all the specifics of the surrounding world; it does not merely obey a rational control or discipline. When I try to harness my body it rebels, like an unbroken horse; it rejects academic instruction. It simply knows better, and I must follow its instinct.

Having left my Kirov tutors, who knew how to subdue my body when it rioted, I became my own coach. I was ruthless with myself; I forced my body into the strict framework of the Vaganova School; I tried to follow her theory to the letter, never allowing a compromise. And suddenly I felt that the control of the Vaganova method was depriving me of my best—it was taking away the freedom of natural, emotional expression, the "singing" character of the movement, the ability to transpose the choreographic design into a human dimension to fill the formal dance grammar with my inner experience. I could breathe freely in the romantic and the neo-classical repertoire, but the rigid form of the classical *Swan Lake* constricted me like a corset. Thus, my first Western performances of *Swan Lake* were far from satisfactory. I was to go through all the choreographies, all the styles (including discotheque dancing), to find an equilibrium between the Vaganova School and a freedom of emotional expression in dance. The fruitful experience of the Kirov needed to be enriched and developed, and I tried my best to achieve this in the West, to justify my rupture with Russia.

I also discovered that the political freedom I had found in the West, the freedom from petty oppression and humiliation, did not automatically warrant artistic freedom. By artistic freedom, I mean being free from any national traditions of dancing, American, Russian, or English; I mean the freedom of synthesis, the freedom to assimilate the best achievements of the world's ballet, the freedom of creation subordinated only to aesthetic criteria. Having defected to the West, I automatically received political freedom, but I still had to fight to win my artistic freedom. And so after my first two years with ABT, I decided to leave it; I felt that my artistic development was outgrowing the repertoire boundaries of the Theatre. It was a difficult decision. I like permanency, I have always disliked a nomadic life, and besides, I felt insecure. I thought, what if no one wants me any more? I kept delaying this step and could have stayed with ABT much longer had it not been for two men who interfered with my life. They were my future husband, Edward Karkar, and Sol Hurok.

Hurok had watched my career attentively from the early 1960's, finding me different from the rest of the Kirov Company. He often came to Leningrad, and once Sergeyev even asked me to accompany Hurok to the airport, where I presented him with a "Russian souvenir"—a jar of homemade salt mushrooms. Later, when I danced at ABT, I learned that he often came to watch me, although he never came to visit me after performances: he was linked with Russia and did not want to endanger his "Russian ballet seasons" by open contacts with a "defector." Once he invited me to meet him in secret at a restaurant in Connecticut (he was a devoted gourmet), and for five hours at dinner he reassured me, saying that I need not leash my dancing career to ABT or to any other Western company, that I was destined to be international, to dance with them all, absorbing all the best there was in the world's ballet and devoting my entire life to it. Hurok added oil to the flame of my doubts and, in the long run, helped me reach the dream of my life: to gain artistic freedom. But it did not happen overnight.

My first two years in the West were a most intense period for me, particularly since my artistic outlook was changing sharply. Sometimes vague feelings in connection with this or that ballet would suddenly come into focus, and my attitude toward it would become clear.

This is what happened with the ballets of Fokine. Formerly I had had an ambiguous attitude toward them. That Fokine is a genius I do not deny, but there are various kinds of genius. One kind outstrips its time, dumbfounding contemporaries with audacious discoveries which become generally accessible only later, possibly much later. The other kind sows the seeds that grow into future developments. The latter, apparently, was the genius of Fokine. Today he is perceived, of necessity, from the perspective of the post-Diaghilev era and of everything of his that is alive in Balanchine, Tudor, Robbins. And alas, no matter how I try in my soul, not one of Fokine's surviving ballets truly affects me, not even *Les Sylphides*, which in Sergeyev's words, was given by God for me to dance.

Partly this is so because, in the West, I somehow stopped loving ballets from the "blue romantic repertoire"; in other words, those works that today seem too "aesthetic." Somehow, an ironic distance sprang up between me and works like the famous *Pas de Quatre*.

Incidentally, in *Pas de Quatre* itself there is a certain irony relating to the competition among the four ballerinas, and if one stresses or emphasizes their eccentricities, the whole style of the work will border on parody. I always sensed this, even at the Kirov, though there I performed *Pas de Quatre* according to the rules of academic schooling. In America I neglected them out of sheer fun. Once in New York I let go completely and danced *Pas de Quatre* with such comedy that the audience choked with laughter. And it happened by itself; before the performance I had no intention of doing any sort of parody. Suddenly, on stage, I felt the extent to which all this mannerism had aged, how it expresses nothing—and involuntarily I changed the accents. As a result, what took place was almost a caricature, for which Clive Barnes took me to task in a review. Well, so what, I got even more satisfaction out of the performance because of that. . . .

With *Les Sylphides* it is different. In *Les Sylphides* there is a unique style. While still, one must always be on the brink of movement. The ballerina, holding an arabesque on pointe, is not poised like a statue, but must seem to be leaning forward, resting in this position only momentarily to flow almost immediately into the next movement. The expression should come from within oneself, conveying the spiritual—something between earth and heaven. And if one runs, one should not seem to touch the ground. In relation to the partner there must be an almost indefinable detachment; ballerina and partner must almost appear not to communicate, and even when expressing some involvement, it should seem to be unreal. The relations between them should maintain this distance and subtlety—all the illusion and delicacy can be destroyed by overstatement or, indeed, by anything obvious.

In America, I lost touch with *Les Sylphides,* partly because I can really dance it only in the Kirov's version; both at the Bolshoi and at Covent Garden, it leaves something to be desired, and at ABT, Fokine's own last version says nothing either to my mind or my heart. Whereas its flaws—the aestheticism that slips easily into a saccharine prettiness I cannot stand—are especially obvious, because the very spirit of Fokine's refined tour de force is alien to the company. They dance it mechanically, without its spirit or its style. Today, in order for *Les Sylphides* to inspire me, to come alive, to agitate from within, I require an absolutely flawless orchestra and, in a stylistic sense, an impeccable entourage. Aesthetic pieces demand perfect beauty and utter purity of execution; otherwise they look simply campy. At ABT, I tried very hard to overcome my predisposition against their version —I substituted the "Prelude" for the "Mazurka," changed my exits, but nothing good came of it. Only once, in America, did I experience real joy from *Les Sylphides.* This was in Philadelphia. The conductor was present at all my rehearsals (when I asked why, he tactfully said, "I come to admire your hands and learn from them"). He interpreted Chopin so brilliantly, with such feeling for rhythm, pauses, and style in general, that I swam in his ambience. I was not dancing to the music, I entered into it and merged with it, almost dissolving in it, and I felt such bliss that I cannot begin to describe it.

I also danced *The Firebird*, which was revived for me at ABT in 1977. *Firebird* is already an archaic ballet, whose antediluvian nature is only heightened by the stunning décor of Natalia Gontcharova and of course by Stravinsky's music. However, Fokine's choreography turned out to be rather difficult for me. On stage, I become exhausted from all the endless combinations of jetés and tours, while sensing their dynamism and particular electricity. This was a technical challenge combined with purely stylistic problems, and I struggled not without enthusiasm. But the style did not finally evoke any feelings at all in me.

It is another matter with Fokine's *The Dying Swan*, which has celebrated its seventieth anniversary by now. Of Fokine's original choreography, however, only scattered fragments remain; as is well known, he created only the bourrées for Pavlova. Subsequently, every performer, be she Ulanova or Plisetskaya or Chauviré, has used the piece to her own taste and at her own risk. In Russia I had danced Dudinskaya's version and never felt myself at home in it. Moreover, I experienced a certain discomfort in front of the audience, from all the sentimental stuff—the rushing around the stage, the flailing of arms, the direct imitation of a dying bird. To the contemporary eye, its conventions look almost ludicrous. When I danced *Dying Swan* for London television, in the autumn of 1970, immediately after my defection, I did feel some satisfaction with it. For one thing, I was dancing only this ballet—it is usually given together with others and you have to conserve your energy—so I was able to concentrate on it completely and enjoy the harmonious simplicity of its choreography and its emotional content.

The Dying Swan has certain specific difficulties: the expressive character of the arms-wings and the free plasticity of the body are combined with continuous bourrées suggesting the movement of a swan gliding on the water. These bourrées look as if the dancer's feet were moving independently from the rest of the body, and at the same time the dance needs total emotional abandon, conveying the image of a struggle with death or a surrender to it. Without this emotional content there can be no drama. What is difficult is that, as I say, the chest and the legs are "divorced" in this dance: the continuous bourrées must be perfectly coordinated with the plasticity of the body thrown into the element of free motion. Otherwise, *The Dying Swan* is not very difficult technically; it is necessary only to rehearse with the arms a lot, and to overcome the tension of the bourrées, which should not exhaust you but come almost mechanically. As for the emotional content, I was helped by Pavlova, whose film of the work I saw. Even today her *Swan* is striking—the flawless feeling for style, the animated face— although certain melodramatic details seem superfluous.

I danced one of my most successful *Swan*s in 1976, in Rio, where my swan had to die twice in one evening. Afterward, Anthony Dowell, with whom I had been dancing a series of pas de deux, came into the dressing room and paid me a compliment that, I thought, was very special. "Oh, what can be done on stage with a pair of beautiful hands, the soul, and the bourrée. Just the soul and the bourrée and nothing else. . . ."

Except for *Petrouchka*, Fokine's other ballets have aged hopelessly. I have seen *Cléopâtra*, and it looks like an oleograph. The same is true of *Schéhérazade*, and it is no accident that it is so seldom revived. His works have already become venerated museum pieces.

September 1972 marked the beginning of my wanderings around the world that continued until I found a haven in London at the Royal Ballet in the summer of 1974. For two years I made almost an Olympic marathon across the world's stages—dozens of *Swan Lake*s and *Giselle*s in South Africa, *The Rite of Spring* (with John Taras' choreography) at La Scala, Stockholm, Munich, Zurich, Paris, *Coppélia* in Berlin. . . . Today I understand that my experiments were uneven, that, probably, a number of them were not worthwhile, but on the whole I profited from them. My stamina developed, and I came to realize more and more clearly what I wanted to do in ballet, both as a dancer and as an actress. It was a time of severe selection. I wasn't jealously holding on to everything I had brought from the Kirov, and yet I wasn't wasting what I had saved from my Russian and American experience. Time was working for me.

One of my most memorable engagements was at the opening of the re-built Reggio Theatre in Turin (it had burned down before World War II). Before this engagement I was a little bit wary of the too tempestuous Italian audience, whose fits of temperament had almost scared me to death at the Scala opening night in 1972. *Un Ballo in Maschera* was given with Placido Domingo, whom from the outset the Milanese treated as if he had fallen flat on his face. They unleashed incredible hubbub in the orchestra—booing, whistling, even throwing apples at him. I had never seen anything like it in my life, and kept wondering what would become of me on the next day when I was supposed to dance *The Rite of Spring*. Fortunately everything had worked out—no booing and no apples.

At the Reggio I danced in Verdi's opera *I Vespri Siciliani*. This was Maria Callas' debut as a director, and she had invited me to perform, having seen me dance somewhere. I never saw Callas on the stage—she never toured in Russia—and by the time of my defection, her operatic career was already over. But I knew her records, and her voice—rather, the human drama contained in the very sound of her voice—had affected me considerably. I had met her previously through my manager, Gorlinsky, who was also hers, and I had visited her at her house in Paris. And I had been completely enthralled by this extraordinary woman—by her directness in conversation, by her intellect, by the absence of any pretentiousness or pose in her, by her elegance, her chic. In daily life she hardly looked to me like that "tigress of the opera" who had lashed out so eccentrically and had once been the center of attention for journalists around the world.

In Turin I danced a one-act ballet, an insertion into Verdi's opera (similar to the "Walpurgis Night" in *Faust*), which Serge Lifar staged for me. The choreography was unpretentious. The seasons of the year were represented, nature's metamorphoses. I was carried in on something like a pedestal, dressed as the goddess Flora in the manner of Botticelli's *La Primavera*, and I danced various things—a lyric mazurka, a bacchanal—in the autumn episode. I became friendly with Lifar—evenings after rehearsals were free and he amused me tremendously with funny stories from his past that he told according to the principle "Se non è vero, ben trovato." His ballet, in spite of its unassuming character, was a success, and in its way it even stood out against the rather grey production, which annoyed Callas no end.

Callas was an actress from head to toe. In her gestures and her manner of holding herself, there was something especially striking. I recall saying to her once that in classical ballet, particularly in the West, very few can use their hands expressively and make them speak. With most dancers, the whole arm moves from the shoulder without the palm opening, which it should, at the end of the movement. This final release of the hands is the dot on the *i* —while using her arms, the ballerina seems to be testing the density of air between them and her body. This is crucial for beautiful port de bras, since the final hand movement is extraordinarily expressive. Used correctly, it can express a great range of emotional shadings, almost an entire character. Maya Plisetskaya often spoke of this in her interviews. For instance, in *Giselle* almost no one can render Bathilde's gesture at that moment when Giselle, with simple-hearted delight, pats the hem of her gold-threaded dress. This gesture should be regal and at the same time a casual "turning with the hand" to Giselle, as if to ask, "What is the matter?" Usually it looks trivial, theatrical, because the hands and the wrists of Western dancers are not utilized properly. "I'm sure you could do this gesture easily," I said to Callas, who instantly performed the very movement with such sovereign grace and simplicity that I was stunned. The turn of the head, the neck, the expression in her eyes—everything came of itself and was absolutely right.

Callas and I spoke at length about art, and when I learned of her sudden death I was not only grieved, as we are grieved by the death of someone we know; I thought of how she had been a rare and, therefore, precious incarnation of natural artistry, whose secret she had taken with her.

I have always remembered what Sergeyev said to me after one of my performances of *Giselle,* in London, in 1970: "I adore you in the romantic ballet, in a romantic tutu, but you have not yet found yourself in a classical tutu!"

To master dancing in both tutus is tantamount to possessing the entire classical legacy of the romantic and Russian academic schools, whose principles inspired the creations of Bournonville, Perrot, and Petipa. I began as a romantic ballerina, but after defecting, I made a firm decision to master the classical tutu.

The romantic tutu demands a special technical approach that is strictly motivated by the stylistics of romantic ballet. They are based on semitones and semiposes, and their understatement is strongly emphasized. The whole poetics of romantic ballet tend to be elusive and indefinite. In order to assimilate this style, one has to have a big, soaring jump, a free-floating torso, as if it were independent from the legs, an indefinable plasticity of the arms—*les bras inachevés*—ethereally sketched in the air, as if testing its density.

The classical tutu, as exemplified by *Swan Lake,* demands more precision in executing classical steps and does not tolerate any romantic elusiveness: all the positions are clearly defined, the extension is bigger, the arabesque and attitude are stretched to the limits, while the torso is absolutely straight. The legs are exposed, all lines are revealed, and you cannot conceal the slightest slip from the audience. The legs must express something: they have a responsibility, so to speak, for your expressiveness, a responsibility they share with the arms. And this expressiveness demands tremendous professionalism, precision in every movement. What is more, classical technique does not permit the relaxed knees that are quite appropriate for the romantic style; it requires an impeccable turn-out, otherwise one cannot achieve any precision in dance phrasing: the lines of the legs will be distorted and lose their beauty. The torso is also differently poised in the classical tutu: it stands on the working leg very firmly, and the sense of center is absolutely definite.

Finally, *Swan Lake* demands from a ballerina quite special physical qualities. It is no coincidence that in the former Maryinsky and in my Kirov, *Swan Lake* was given only to those ballerinas who possessed these qualities: soft, flowing lines of the body, long legs, expressive, elongated arms with a specific relaxation at the elbow, a clearly pronounced arch. And so certain ballerinas who could be perfect in *Giselle* or *Sleeping Beauty,* but who didn't meet these specific physical requirements, never got the chance to attempt *Swan Lake:* for instance, Irina Kolpakova and Alla Sizova at the Kirov. Whereas Maya Plisetskaya, well known for her flowing line, danced Myrtha, never Giselle, since the romantic style per se was not her forte.

In *Swan Lake,* as in *Giselle,* the second act is the key to the ballet and the most difficult in terms of style and dramatic expressiveness. But if in the second act of *Giselle* it is essential to overcome the "par terre" by soaring over the stage, for *Swan Lake* this springy, big jump is not necessary.

ve left: With Lucia Chase, after Baryshnikov's first ABT performance, July 27, 1974

tom left: Curtain call for EPILOGUE, with Erik Bruhn

right: With Maria Callas, Turin

tom right: New York State Theatre

What's more important is the flexibility of the body and the "singing" lines of the arms. Besides, in *Swan Lake* you have to feel the ground under your feet: this is the earth, a glade by a lake, where Odette is stretching out her wings as if testing her ability to take flight—a metaphor of her captive spirit, thrusting to freedom.

Technically this ballet is much more difficult for me than *Giselle*, because its basis is an intricate academic dance, fostered by Petipa and Lev Ivanov. You cannot perform its patterns differently every time: each sissonne or rond de jambe is to be executed according to the specific academic canon, established by Petipa. Due to my natural impulsiveness that sometimes makes me surrender my control over my body, I find myself involuntarily attempting to dance the given classical patterns differently each time. I seem to be trying to escape from that precision of movement which is utterly essential for Petipa's style. In Russia I had not worked on *Swan Lake* very much, and therefore its mechanical technique, implying the ability of the body to perform the same classical combinations again and again with the same precision and the same attack, never became organic to me.

In its dramatic aspect, *Swan Lake* is a real challenge compared to *The Sleeping Beauty* or *Giselle*. *Sleeping Beauty* is a *ballet féerie*, a fairy tale, devoid of the dramatic conflict with which *Swan Lake* abounds. *Sleeping Beauty* is a triumph of academic virtuosity, permeated with a youthful charm which a ballerina has to radiate. *Swan Lake* is a lyrical drama in dance requiring not only impeccable academic schooling but a special gift for dramatic acting. *Giselle* is a more aesthetic ballet, more conventional, because the naïveté of the plot gives it a certain primitive charm that excludes the genuine tragedy of human existence. Only the second act is truly dramatic—the first is a bit old-fashioned. And there is really nothing to say about the music; Adolphe Adam wrote tunes to dance to, nice for the feet, but capable of offending the ear with their operatic manner, especially to people trained on Wagner, Brahms, or Stravinsky. (The music is, after all, of the same period as Offenbach.) This is music *to which* one dances.

With Tchaikovsky, it is a matter of music *in which*—or *beyond which*—one dances. It leads you; it subordinates you to itself; it is almost beyond the ability of the body, as it makes each note concrete, to compete with it. *Swan Lake* has survived the test of time because the choreography of the ballet frequently rises to the level of the genius of Tchaikovsky's music—especially Ivanov's second act, an absolute masterpiece. The last act is, unfortunately, rather illustrative, attaining real drama and meaning for me only in John Cranko's version. I keep waiting for someone with the talent and the daring to take and read the score with fresh eyes, but to do this after Ivanov is horribly difficult. Indeed, even the finale can be worked out quite differently: what if, let's say, Siegfried kills Rothbart and perishes himself, redeeming the betrayal and paying for Odette's freedom?

Attempts have been made to interpret *Swan Lake* as a psychological drama occurring entirely within Siegfried's soul, with the image of Odette perceived only as his dream of a romantically lofty love, a last fantasy of his youthful mind to which he is bidding farewell as he enters his maturity. Odette's death is equated with the loss of youthful purity, to be followed by a wise acceptance of the prose of life, incompatible with dreams. Thus was *Swan Lake* conceived by Yury Grigorovich at the Bolshoi, but the Party ignoramuses considered his version too pessimistic, and did not allow him to realize it.

Swan Lake's meaning is unique, because through the contours of an old fairy tale the reality of life surfaces—the truth about its imperfection, about pining for true love and love's unfulfillment, which can be realized only in death (the Wagnerian idea of *Liebestod,* the idea of *Tristan).*

For me, Act II is the key. It reveals the core of the drama as well as the ballet's essence—the nature and fate of Odette.

Over many years I have read Odette differently: as a frightened, fluttering bird-maiden, in whom love for Siegfried calls human feelings to life. At the last, she awakens to the understanding that she is to be denied love by her fate. Later, I softened the bird-like features and mannerisms, got rid of the excessive fluttering, and concentrated entirely on Odette's human nature. This was another extreme that was not too satisfying to me. I wanted to find a golden mean—and I believe I finally found it. Odette is an enchanted bird-maiden who knows her fate; the Prince does not know it, but she does. She knows that the desire for love, which is inexhaustible in any living creature, the belief in love, must be marked by the trauma of failure. There is wisdom in Odette, wisdom deriving from hopelessness, from a kind of severe, penetrating view of life, but wisdom does not console; knowledge prolongs suffering—it does not alleviate it.

I hear all of this in Tchaikovsky's music. Tchaikovsky is a desperate perfectionist and therefore he is constantly disillusioned; his music is full of this romantic longing for love. It resounds in the central theme of *Swan Lake* and in the growth of the Christmas tree in *The Nutcracker,* and in all the bitterness springing from the knowledge that it is not given for one's ideal love to come into existence. These feelings are very close to me personally, and the music of *Swan Lake* says all of this to me.

In the finale, Odette is happy that she has forgiven Siegfried, happy because she has learned to forgive. This is the lesson of her love—she has acquired a human characteristic which she had not known previously and which was awakened by love. In this I see love's greatest gift: its power to purify and transform the soul. Forgiveness is more powerful than death and transcends it; it carries Odette above the cares of the world, the crafty ruses of Rothbart, and Siegfried's weakness. Odette is united with her Prince in the world beyond, wiser still, because she has come to know certain boundaries—the ultimate truth about life.

Rehearsing with Rudolf Nure

My Odette, the one I imagine, I can dance only in the Russian tradition of cantilena. Unlike many Western ballerinas, I do not in my mind break Tchaikovsky's music into measures. I do not count them, and neither do I worry about exactly fixing every position against the music or "freezing" the arabesques and attitudes. That way is, of course, quite a showy way of dancing, but in *Swan Lake* I feel that such sensationalism is all but fatal, tearing, as it does, the continuity of the choreographic texture to the detriment of its meaning. Is not the white adagio a *story* Odette tells of her captivity, of her hopes, her fears? Like any story, it requires that the narration be fluent. This is why I divide Tchaikovsky's music into phrases, not measures, trying to sing them. That is the way I was trained at the Vaganova School and at the Kirov. My way is to sing with my dancing, to make the movement itself last and finally extend itself, to "draw" the ballet phrase the way a singer "holds" the note. And this is much harder than finishing each step on the note.

Not everybody in the West approves of this distinctive Russian bel canto in dancing; many people regard it as anti-musical. For me, though, breaking of the music into separate measures is merely mechanical and thwarts the proper cantilena style of *Swan Lake*.

For all the choreographic complexity of the part, Odette suits my dance characteristics: I know that if my feet should let me down, my natural lyricism and acquired artistic habits would rescue me. I would recover, not "fall apart" on stage. Odile is another matter. I never feel sure of myself in her tutu, because for many years the choreographic outline of the part did not feel comfortable. I had no confidence in it but forced myself into it and so couldn't find the proper state of mind. There is nothing vampish about me, and it is not natural for me to play a seductress or a *femme fatale*. In Odile, I have had to discover, as an actress, that which my own nature does not possess: aggressiveness, bravado, a glory in one's own triumph. For me, Odile was like a wall of glass which I was always trying to scramble over, getting my hands bloody. This was a tremendous challenge, and it took years to overcome the barriers. I have constantly sought that inner truth that would help me find in Odile's character something similar to mine—or I would never feel comfortable in her choreography.

At first, despite all my efforts, I couldn't get rid of her traditional image, the stereotyped, one-dimensional Bad Woman. Odile became more understandable for me when I managed to see in her the mysterious stranger, reminiscent of those *femmes fatales* from the romantic poetry of Alexander Blok. I imagined her as an enchantress out of nowhere, whose ambiguous past makes her inaccessible to anyone. Odile suddenly became surrounded with a mysterious aura. But everything mysterious is not alien to me, and she emerged in my mind as a beautiful woman quite conscious of her vicious charms and her liaison with evil. According to the libretto, she is Rothbart's daughter, but I chose to disregard this convention. She might just as well be his ally, employing her natural wickedness in her own manner and to her own ends. Like Odette, she knows her destiny—to charm people with her supernatural destructive beauty, then to keep those who fall victim to it at a distance, never giving herself to them. She is playing with Siegfried, just as she has done with others—for the sake of her own amusement, in order to prove her irresistibility once again. Rothbart merely provides her with the chance to assert her evil. This approach has made Odile psychologically more understandable for me (and, I hope, more convincing for the audience). And it is no accident that some people prefer me now as Odile rather than Odette. This means that artistic and technical qualities acquired through hard work may sometimes actually appear more convincing, even stronger, to the public than innate ones.

Sometimes I am told that I have complete mastery in *Swan Lake*. But that feeling is entirely alien to me, for mastery implies something rigid, almost petrified—something hostile to art, the enchantment of which lies in its spontaneity, in the unpredictability of its movement. Of course, in *Swan Lake* I have acquired by now a certain amount of experience, certain particularly technical habits: now I am less vulnerable to the external world, to its distracting influences. I have stopped fighting with this ballet.

In spite of this, *Swan Lake* constantly demands tremendous physical preparation, which is unnecessary, for instance, for *Giselle*. Each time, *Swan Lake* convinces me that our balletic life is a struggle for the retention of what has already been discovered—the technique we pursue as if it were the Firebird. It is the most elusive thing on earth, and in *Swan Lake*, if it suddenly disappears, no amount of "interpretation" will help.

I do not know when it was exactly—probably the winter of 1977 with ABT in New York—that I was dancing *Giselle* for the nth time and suddenly all my disorganized thoughts about it settled down and formed themselves into a coherent structure. It was as if someone had poured some kind of liquid into the suspended solution of my thoughts; the solution cleared and the sediment settled. I suddenly understood why the plot itself had never excited me: the poor village girl, the count pretending to be a peasant and deceiving her, insanity, death—the whole ordinary little melodrama, interpreted and re-interpreted a thousand times and by now completely uninteresting. Beyond the primitive plot I suddenly had a clear vision—not just of a romantic drama, but of a drama of the dualism of body and spirit, of their fatal incompatibility, which turns out to be the tragedy of love.

And this tragedy lies in the fact that if a union of the lovers is possible on the physical or everyday level, then it will never be achieved on the

Rehearsing with Anthony Dowell

spiritual plane, and vice versa. In the first act the lovers are happy, but they cannot be united in the flesh (it doesn't really matter why). In the second act, a complete spiritual union takes place, but beyond the grave, alien to the flesh, in the isolation of the forest. For me, as Giselle in the second act, it is not important whether I am a romantic phantom, merging into a circle dance of Wilis obeying the will of their queen, Myrtha, or whether I am the product of Albrecht's feverish imagination awakened by repentance, as Mischa Baryshnikov interprets it.

Only one thing is important to me: both acts of *Giselle* are manifestations of her soul, her inner states of being. And her soul is one. In the first act, still in her corporeal existence, she lives with ordinary human concerns—the dances with the villagers, the suitor, Hilarion, the meeting with the count and with Bathilde, the unmasking of Albrecht, her madness—which are transformed in her by the first feelings of love. But freedom from these wearying realities comes with death. In the second act, her soul, freed of all that is worldly, superficial, and ordinary, is filled with regal quietude and wisdom, and she becomes a bearer of eternal femininity, of chastity and purity. And in this purity she is not capable of punishing; she is now above the earthly passions and their excitements. Only forgiveness is available to her, and it comes to her naturally, from her deep feminine sympathy.

Having acquired this angle of vision, I could assimilate the entire role. Today I do not need to work up a mood or ask my friends: "How would you like to see me do it tonight?" I have found the general contours, laid the groundwork, and the necessary inner state comes of itself. Formerly I was always in search of it, because without it I am never able to justify each balletic position and gesture, I cannot make a movement natural. Within the framework of this general outline, I now can vary the shading like a painter, adding or taking away a color here and there, darkening or lightening the play of shadow and light. But the picture in its general aspect is already clear.

Now, for me, there is no break between the first and the second acts—the first leads into the second. In her quite real peasant world, Giselle is an odd girl, "not of this world," not entirely in contact with others; she lives more within herself. Any exaggerated expressions and jumping about are inappropriate—gesture is kept to a minimum, implying a strict reserve. It is as if fate has drawn an enchanted circle around my village girl, and will not allow her to break out of it. This restraint may seem puzzling, as if Giselle has some hidden secret, or as if an unseen ailment is gnawing at her. So it *should* seem. Giselle is marked by a romantic destiny; she is special, not ordinary. And an early death is preordained for her.

Of my former exuberant Giselle, excessively down-to-earth and therefore quite incorrect outside the style and romantic intent of the ballet, there remains not a trace. I have removed other colors, too, things I used even recently—extreme fearfulness, girlish shyness—which would look old-fashioned and entirely uninteresting now. And this oddness, this special-ness, about Giselle also restructures the second act, both its accents and its essence.

The most difficult thing about the second act is to feel that I am not a body any more, but a spirit. And yet to play a spirit is impossible; what is necessary is to project another essence from inside the transition. This is an initiation into something supernatural, beyond the boundary of reason. In me the feeling for the mystical is very strong; I can almost physically sense "communion" with the supernatural. Standing on the steps of Giselle's grave, with my arms crossed like those of a dead person—this is a leitmotif of the Wilis, a gesture both strange and ordinary in nature and therefore very helpful in finding the necessary internal state—I imagine myself a participant in a rite, a mystery. I always experience a very sharp, plaintive feeling when, with her magical sprig of mistletoe, Myrtha forces my spirit—the spirit of Giselle—to move. The first, the second, the third almost weightless step, and then I have begun to spin on the spot, like a genie freed from a bottle. The combination of leaps demonstrates vividly the desire of my Giselle to break away from the stage, to overcome her link with the earth, to soar.

The complexity of the second act is in the terre à terre movements. It is necessary to overcome the sense of being tied to the earth; to imbue every-thing with weightlessness, lightness, and simplicity.

Simplicity is important—unusually so—to Giselle's liberated soul, rev-eling in the moonlit night; to the silence of the burial ground; to her inter-nal peace. Any contrivance of pose or stylistic extreme is alien. But this simplicity is incompatible with the refined elegance of Taglioni's lithographs which I admired at one time: that uniquely turned neck, a stricture in the taste of the turn of the century—the way I looked in the posters of the Ki-rov Theatre, the way the public and I myself once liked to see me.

For a long time, I was unable to part with these French tricks. My coach, Maggie Black, helped me, at one of our rehearsals of the second act. "There's something undefined in these poses of yours," she noted quite penetratingly. They were undefined because they did not correspond to my new internal state. In the Kirov, when I was a different person, they had suited me well. Now I was uncomfortable in them and it was immediately noticeable. So I stopped worrying about them and simply did what was called for. I realized that austerity and simplicity are what I require today, for they allow me to find in my Giselle that inner peace and that deep con-centration which appear to me essential. The problem of whether to forgive or not to forgive, over which I had racked my brains for so long, fell away of itself—not because Giselle could not act otherwise, but because *I* could not, as I can only love my deceiver Albrecht.

Having undertaken to stage "The Kingdom of the Shades" scene from
La Bayadère, I honestly did not recall the choreography at first. It was like
a nightmare for the whole three months. Bits and pieces came to mind
when and how they pleased—in the elevator, in bed before sleep, at
breakfast, at rehearsals when I was supposed to be thinking about another
ballet entirely. I put it together from fragments, recording things on videotape, and gradually I came up with a patchwork quilt, a mosaic. It was
devilishly tense work, and I worried terribly. With justification.

First of all, I did not know how to place my twenty-four girls of the
corps on the stage instead of the thirty-two shades who were necessary for
Petipa's geometrically constructed composition. Tudor suggested a design
that he created with extreme precision, but nothing positive came out of it.
I decided to place my girls by eye, relying upon my own sense of stage
space to re-create the essence of Petipa's pattern.

By staging "The Kingdom of the Shades" I was taking a kind of examination. Not only did I have to convince people of what I had learned at the
Vaganova School and the Kirov, but to prove to myself that I was able to
teach other ballerinas Petipa's style, which had never entirely been assimi-
lated by them before. Besides, my English was far from adequate for explaining to the girls at ABT the subtleties of *Bayadère*'s style and to work
them into the peculiarities of the Russian tradition of execution.

The style of *Bayadère* reveals the artistry of the early Petipa. It is still
far from the intricate choreographic harmony of *Sleeping Beauty* or Ivanov's
impressionistic palette, whose colors diversify the second act of *Swan Lake.*
The refined simplicity and purity of geometric composition that dominate
the style of "Shades" must be transformed into poetry through inspired performance. It is essentially the pure poeticized classical dancing whose
beauty and harmony are amalgamated at the heart of Russian schooling. To
create this refined beauty through dancing is exceedingly hard, since each
movement has to be impeccably executed in complete accordance with the
academic canon.

Dancing "Shades" used to give me enormous enjoyment when I opened
a hand correctly, or closed a fifth position clearly, or stretched a leg flaw-
lessly in arabesque. But this enjoyment is not an end in itself; it can
merely stimulate the execution of steps, bordering on simple class exercises, if they are not poetically extended—if they are not carried into another dimension motivated by the content of *Bayadère.* The sense of this
was not so obvious to my girls as it was to me, who held in memory the
whole production of *Bayadère* that I had danced so often at the Kirov.

Actually the "Shades" are only part of the entire picture of *Bayadère*—
the visions, elicited by opium smoking, in the mind of the warrior Solor,
who is tormented by repentance and love for the dead bayadère, Nikiya.
These shades are essentially romantic creatures, though they are not
dressed in the romantic tutu (which through its very appearance usually

evokes an otherworldly image) but clad in the classic one, which by itself totally commits dancers to the classical style. And so "Shades" provides a double stylistic difficulty: here is a classic, but it has a slight romantic tone. "Shades" is a distinctive tribute by Petipa to the sylphides and nymphs of the old romantic ballet, whose supernatural features are now to emerge through the means of purely classical ballet as fostered by Petipa. *Bayadère* does not abound in soaring jumps, and its mysterious ambience is not to be evoked by elusive tilts of the torso, or through hopping flights across the stage. It is to be achieved by overcoming the earthbound choreographic pattern in spite of its nonromantic tutu.

"Shades" is performed against a backdrop, from behind which the girls emerge, one after another. And the audience sees Petipa's whole composition as pure abstraction. So I must explain to my charges that they are meant to be walking out of some kind of crevice or grotto over which hover the dismal rocks. The first step of each shade-ballerina is the arabesque directed forward, after which a shade steps back, stretching her arms backward as if the mysterious darkness of the grotto still draws her. And this arabesque is repeated by all the girls as they fill the stage space. Under Petipa the shades were illuminated by day lighting: the choreographer cancelled the ubiquitous romantic moon, because, to his mind, the dancing *on its own* was supposed to convey the physical feeling of night air as well as the entire mysterious atmosphere of a no-man's land.

I felt very embarrassed at explaining these subtleties to the girls. At the first rehearsal, my legs were giving way beneath me from fear, my voice quivered, but nevertheless the girls somehow understood me. More than that, they listened with unflagging attention and followed my every movement.

I had to dance for everyone and explain what kind of expressive implications each arabesque should have, how one can express through the same basic movement either a thrusting impetus or a majestic quiet. I told them that in each ballet the arabesque may have a different meaning, depending on the music, the ballet style, and the plot. And how dancers can convey these differences if they grasp the coloration of each scene and make their bodies respond to it. Before, the girls at ABT had never been taught to pass every movement through the body, to "eat it up," as we used to say in the Vaganova School. But I was struck by how quickly they grasped these things, which were commonplace for me yet equivalent to a revelation for them.

They obediently followed my instructions and I was immensely grateful to them. Their spirit of cooperation helped my monstrous tension gradually abate. Of course, I took the Kirov ensemble in its best years as the stylistic tuning fork, those years when the geometric compositions of Petipa were filled with meaning and true inspiration.

earsing GISELLE

With Anthony Dowell

I was attempting to achieve a feeling of ensemble by saying to my girls that each of them ought to be the shadow of a solo ballerina, that each was a soloist in miniature, a nuance at play within the ballet's choreographic spectrum. I worked individually with almost everyone, making each of the girls conscious of her strong and weak sides. And with the help of Dina Makarova, I recorded my rehearsals on videotape. After each rehearsal I would play the tape, noting the flaws of each individual shadow. In this way I worked day and night. After playing the tape I would often polish some passages with Dina; sometimes, like two frenzied bacchantes, we tossed about between the two beds in my hotel bedroom checking each position, changing it, and making it precise. In the morning I would arrive at ABT and explain to each girl whatever was not right, and immediately we would clear up any blemishes.

This meticulous work on *La Bayadère* was gradually transformed into a true creative enjoyment for me. My charges turned out to be very quick to imitate, and it amazed me that when I was no longer rehearsing with them, they themselves taught new girls in the same stylistic key that I had given them. I am grateful to Michael Lland, an ABT ballet master, who watched all my rehearsals and, thanks to his exceptional memory, remembered everything in detail. He has carried on my work beautifully, never letting the troupe slide. Alas, they could lose their new habits very easily: they didn't have them deep in the body's memory; their muscles reacted differently from mine, being trained more mechanically—or more formally, if you will.

After mutual understanding had been established at rehearsals and I stopped being embarrassed, a genuine creative atmosphere sprang into being. I shouted at them, was demanding, dissatisfied, approving—in short, everything was as it should be.

The situation with Nikiya's part was even more complicated. Nikiya's choreographic pattern does not in itself suggest otherworldliness. Even the plasticity of Giselle's spirit in Act II is more concrete than Nikiya's. Giselle is, at least, active; she is doing all she can to keep Albrecht alive. In *La Bayadère* the sense of Nikiya coming from the other world is arrived at solely by means of her physical image and those overtones a ballerina can introduce into her plasticity. While working with Martine van Hamel and Cynthia Gregory, I used to tell them that Nikiya seems to incarnate Solor's suffering, his pangs of conscience and anguish for his thwarted love. The dancer's face should bear no sign of emotion; the feelings Solor is flooded with are expressed only by Nikiya's body. Like a cello, it sings out with its every movement what the hero is tormented by, since the phantom Nikiya is merely a figment of his imagination. It is absolutely necessary to combine in Nikiya's image the perfection of technique with a serene detachment that promises the forgiveness for which Solor yearns.

Owing to her temperament, Martine used to accentuate her virtuosity and lose the lucid austerity of the image. I would make her soften the emphasis and smooth the transitions, and ultimately she did well. The most difficult task is to grasp the mystical mood permeating Nikiya's first pas de deux with Solor. If the dancer fails to sense the liturgical character of their encounter, the whole set of développés à la seconde and tours seems like a simple class exercise, for in this pas de deux Nikiya must seem to be divulging the mysteries of the other world to Solor. The opening of the leg à la seconde, for instance, should be performed like opening a missal, or praying. This spiritual mood has to be felt, or else one cannot convey the special lucidity that informs Petipa's compositions.

It was very difficult for me personally to dance Nikiya, since my responsibility to myself and to the girls was greatly increased. Having demanded stylistic flawlessness from them, I was obliged to set a certain example, and that limited my freedom. Therefore, my first performances of *La Bayadère* were far from perfect. I didn't forgive myself the slightest error, I was nervous, my body would not obey, because I did not possess that internal freedom without which it is impossible in the dance to achieve even an approximation of perfection.

At the premiere of *La Bayadère*, danced by Cynthia Gregory, I was as agitated as I had ever been in my life. Pale, shaking, with sweaty hands, I sat in the audience next to Tudor. And when the first shade-girl started to wobble in an écarté (things like this, as is well known, are contagious and can quickly spread to the entire corps de ballet), I was ready to die from fear. At this point, Tudor poured oil on the flames. "Look, look, this is only the beginning. Soon they'll all start shaking," he whispered, not without malignant joy. (It's true that Antony later said ABT's corps de ballet had never danced so magnificently.) Happily, it was a false alarm, and when the "parade of shades" was over and they started to disappear from the stage there was a burst of applause. My girls had won; even the perfectly turned-out fifth position, over which we had killed ourselves, did not slip once. When the premiere went well and even the exacting Arlene Croce called the performance "Makarova's miracle" (to my chagrin), I did not so much feel relief from the tension under which I had lived for the previous months as a great renewed confidence in the rightness of the principles of the Russian school.

In the summer of 1974, after *La Bayadère*, I joined the Royal Ballet as a permanent guest artist. This move to England was my second defection, as it were; this time from ABT. I was not going to dissolve my relationship with the company, but organize it on a different basis. At the Royal I found myself in a creative situation very different from that in America. Everything was less hectic and exhausting, more poised and marked with dis-

Staging LA BAYADÈRE

left: Coaching Kim Highton in LA BAYADÈRE

right: With Antony Tudor

om: Opening night curtain call for LA BAYADÈRE

tinguished taste. After the Babel-like confusion of styles at ABT, with its extreme versatility, the English atmosphere with its refined stylistic distinction had a wholesome effect on me. Englishmen are proud of their deeply organic sense of style.

Before 1974 I had frequently danced with the Royal as a guest artist. On one occasion, I was invited to take part in a gala performance for the Queen; I was to dance a pas de deux from *Swan Lake* with Donald MacLeary. Numerous reporters and photographers came to watch the dress rehearsal—they organized a press-call, and I was dancing on a high emotional note. It was my second performance before the London audience I had loved since my "defection tour" with the Kirov. But I had bad luck: at the rehearsal, doing a jeté entrelacé, I badly injured a thigh muscle. The pain was overwhelming, I could not keep myself from crying out, but my scream was drowned in the roar of the orchestra: the conductor noticed nothing. Overcoming the pain, I stumbled to the wings; Ninette de Valois rushed to help me, and they carried me to the dressing room. Thus, the renewal of my contact with the Royal began under an unfavorable sign, and for a while, it seemed, it was a meaningful omen.

Our relations became complicated. To tell the truth, neither *Giselle* nor *Sleeping Beauty* nor *Les Sylphides* brought me a real success in London before 1974. They were not failures, but I was not at all satisfied with my performances. Six months after the gala in which I never danced, in 1972, I appeared at Covent Garden again—twice in *Giselle* with Anthony Dowell, twice in *Swan Lake* with MacLeary, and in *Les Sylphides* and a pas de deux from *Don Quixote*, both with Dowell. These performances did not bring me any joy either. I had the feeling that the London audience was also slightly disappointed. When I started rehearsing *Giselle* in New York during the Royal tour in May 1972, I was disturbed that I could not develop any contact with Dowell. Like the rest of the company, he treated me with a certain caution and a reserved politeness, seeing in me another "Russian ballet star." I wanted a simple and direct human contact, but my attempts were thwarted by his shyness and his British restraint. I constantly had the feeling that he was afraid of abandoning this official tone, of making a faux pas, and that paralyzed both of us. The same strained politeness was still there in our relationship when I came to London in June, and it made me uneasy.

Besides, the English production of *Giselle* did not seem to me convincing at all: it abounded with sweet *paysannerie* and boring pantomime, illustrating all kinds of rubbish such as, "It's time to wake up Mommy," and so on; the lighting was so bad that we literally danced in the dark. And my slightly "Americanized" *Giselle* was not accepted in London by those who knew my former Kirov performances. My extreme emotional directness in acting, my exaggerated impulsiveness that corresponded to Kirov traditions, sometimes seemed in America an overstatement. Our perceptions and cultural backgrounds were very different, and I had to take them into consideration, so in America I had to fill in the outline of my Giselle, make her less poetic and refined, more "earthbound." I started to accent her sickliness and not the strangeness of her nature. In the first act I would grasp my heart, indicating an assault of dizziness as if to give a realistic basis for her death from nervous shock.

The whole approach seemed a bit too black and white, and I subsequently rejected it. At this time, those who had liked my previous interpretation said that my new approach was "not sufficiently aesthetic." They discerned the loss of the Russian nuances and details of execution, the whole poetic tradition of interpretation, which London had loved since the time of Ulanova's tours. "Why did you exaggerate the drama so? It should only be sketched in." Now I understand that they were right. Besides, at my first performance some little things happened that distressed me. For instance, I was startled by the dead silence following my entry in Act II. In America my promenade en arabesque usually evoked the applause of a public reacting in a more spontaneous way. In London they did not applaud, according to their etiquette that does not allow them to interrupt the cantilena of a performance. In short, my first Royal Ballet experience with *Giselle* was far from perfect.

Everything went better with *Swan Lake:* in contrast to Anthony, MacLeary did not display an excessive piety to a visiting prima. Besides, after a "marathon" in South Africa, I had grown much stronger technically and was surer of myself. *Swan Lake* was my only happy moment in that London tour in the summer of 1972.

Success and inner satisfaction came with my new works at Covent Garden—*Romeo and Juliet* in 1973, *Manon* and *The Song of the Earth* in 1974, all by Kenneth MacMillan. The Royal had offered me the best they possessed. But the two *Sleeping Beauty*s I danced with Rudi—my first *Sleeping Beauty* in the West—proved an exhausting introduction to those new ballets.

I had never attempted *The Sleeping Beauty* since my Kirov tour to Japan in 1969, and then I danced it without adequate preparation, almost *à l'improviste;* and so I never had a real chance on this ballet. I rehearsed the final pas de deux with Rudi for a few days, but, of course, the performance was not free of serious flaws.

Nicolas Sergeyev's production differed from the Kirov version in its staccato style, at the expense of the smooth legato I was familiar with. Probably, this version was truer to the old St. Petersburg choreography, since at the Kirov *The Sleeping Beauty* had passed through the hands of many choreographers, such as Fedor Lopukhov, who choreographed the first variation of the Lilac Fairy, and Konstantin Sergeyev, who cleaned up the obsolete pantomime episodes. In the Royal, however, there were other innovations, like Aurora's second-act variation choreographed by MacMillan in the style of Petipa, with a subtle hint of neo-classical movement. I grew fond of it at once, preferring it to the familiar Petipa variation.

Some episodes in the Royal's *Beauty* I performed in my own way: for instance, in Aurora's entry I did grands jetés according to the Russian tradition; since Vaganova developed the grand jeté in female dancing, it has become an integral element of the Russian style, and the grands jetés reveal much more of the playfulness of the sixteen-year-old princess than the former tiny pas de chat. In fact, all of Aurora's variations, except for the one by MacMillan that I liked so much, I danced in accordance with the Kirov standard. There was one hitch: the famous fish dives that crowned the final pas de deux of Aurora and Florimund. In Russia we used to do pirouettes *en dedans* at this point, while in the West, since the time of Olga Spessivtseva, this very spectacular support has been in use. But I could not seem to perfect it. Essentially, it's just a trick demanding an elaborate preparation and a special knack in the distribution of energy. Accustomed to the pirouettes, I would use too strong a force for the "fish" and, as a result, at the performance the "fish" was slurred and the critics reproved me. Later, I spent a lot of time with Ivan Nagy working on this tour de force before I learned how to achieve it in a more or less acceptable way.

Another stumbling block for my Aurora became the purely English accents in Aurora's Rose Adagio with the four cavaliers, born from the musically precise style of the London *Sleeping Beauty*. According to the English tradition, modeled after Margot Fonteyn, each of Aurora's attitudes was to end on the last note of the measure. Such timing brought a particular swift effect to the momentary positioning. I felt, however, that this effect broke the legato and special continuity of the choreographic texture that seems to be stretching along with the slow music by Tchaikovsky. In the Kirov we never timed the positions exactly to the music. We simply "grew" into the attitudes, often holding beyond the note, but always preserving the general ligature of the choreography, maybe sometimes even exaggerating it. My finishes beyond the note looked anti-musical in comparison with the lightning precision of Margot, who froze in an attitude exactly on the accent. . . . Of course, I could not change my habits and acquire this precision in the few available rehearsals, and therefore I postponed the polishing of the effect to a later time.

When I remember now my 1973 Royal tour, I am amazed that I survived with *Sleeping Beauty* followed by *Romeo and Juliet*—which I had to learn in a week! If three years earlier somebody had told me that in the West ballet performances were cooked up at such speed, I would never have believed it. But the years in the West had helped me develop a very special concentration, an ability to focus all my will, which I had never had in Russia, where everything flowed in a calm way, stretching through many months of probing rehearsals.

Above: With Anthony Dowell

Right: Rehearsing MANON
with Anthony Dowell

I worked on MacMillan's Juliet with Georgina Parkinson, who literally showed me every step. And I had no trouble with the choreography, learning the order of steps even faster than usual. I abandoned Lavrovsky's version very easily, because it was obliterated in my body's memory, although MacMillan's approach to Prokofiev's music reminded me somewhat of Lavrovsky's. Both of them were oriented toward a "ballet drama" abounding in pantomime. Both revealed a certain tendency to illustrate Shakespeare too directly. Because of these similarities I was not immediately impressed by MacMillan's choreography when I saw it first in New York and then in London in 1972: I did not fully appreciate its contemporary language and its invention. The modern vocabulary and vision made themselves felt most strongly in the enticing and very intricate pas de deux, but in performance, I was overcome by Romeo-Rudi, who was utterly passionate, untrammeled in his feelings, almost driven by an insanity of sensual desire. His dancing was magnificent, fresh, without even the slightest technical flaws. In the death scene he jumped upon the platform in front of Juliet's tomb like a wounded beast, and I suddenly was struck almost physically by his inner state. Juliet-Margot seemed to me too reserved. I felt something cerebral in her approach to the part, a certain holding back prevailing over the impulses of passion. Therefore in my work on Juliet I pushed myself away from Margot and used Ulanova as a stylistic model.

It is curious that, in the beginning, I found MacMillan's choreography uncomfortable, owing to its unusual approach and combinations. And I had the same feeling later on working on *Manon*. However, after I entered his style (which happened quite soon), everything went well. A "peculiar cantilena of angularities" was born, and it actually helped me realize my dramatic resources rather than hindered them. After the very first rehearsal I knew Juliet was a role for me, and I felt I would be good in it. I knew the music well, and I was not disturbed even when I had to rehearse without Rudi (who, as usual, had some parallel engagements in Europe). Even the pas de deux I learned with Georgina, who was extremely generous and never seemed to tire of helping me. I met my Romeo-Rudi for the first time at the dress rehearsal, when I jumped out on stage with an intricate Renaissance hairdo that did not go well with my small figure. I sensed that Rudi was startled at the sight, and the whole rehearsal turned into one continuous misunderstanding: I mixed up my entrances, all the scenery was unsteady, the balcony almost broke under my feet. But somehow I was sure that at the performance everything would fall into place. Contact with Rudi was established immediately: at the end of the first act, in the balcony scene, I rushed down the stairs to meet Romeo, and when he caught my hand, I was astounded by the boyish infatuation and the passion that emanated from Rudi. He gave me immense emotional impetus, and we did not even have to act; we simply became the lovers of Verona.

Later, with each of my Romeos—Rudi, Anthony, Mischa—I felt a little different; each of them seemed to touch different sides of my soul, and my Juliet was different with each of them. With Rudi I felt like the younger lover, more naïve and inexperienced, and the energy he radiated charged me with mad romanticism. With the more vulnerable and lyrical Anthony, who was a boy on stage rather than a man, I felt like an elder sister, prepared to take care of him and defend him. The part became more serene; in the same balcony scene, in the pas de deux, I enjoyed a light joy at the unfamiliar feelings enveloping me rather than the passion and the madness of love that had permeated me with Rudi. I remember the Metropolitan Opera House performance with Anthony in May 1976: how easy the excruciating jetés on pointe became for me. I had the physical feeling of tearing the air apart—I subdued the space to the dance that filled all my being. Nothing else existed for me, an emotional upsurge possessed me, and there were no difficulties; all those exhausting jetés seemed a continuation, even a result, of my inner state.

When I danced the same scene with Mischa at a gala in Washington, I was carried away by the infinite emotion; it was like a spark coming from the contact of opposite electrical charges. Mischa was all in a transport of passion, the incarnation of young ardor, sensual and ecstatic. And we danced as one human being, which does not happen often. It seemed as if I took one breath at the beginning of the pas de deux, and it was enough for the whole dance. Mischa was superb, and if with Dowell I responded to his tenderness, with Baryshnikov I was driven by an emotional madness brought to the limits of human capacity.

At approximately the same time as *Manon,* I began to work on *The Song of the Earth.* This ballet had one rare and precious quality: MacMillan's choreography was remarkably suited to the music of Mahler's "symphony of songs," and they both struck a deep response in my soul. I spent many hours listening to the music and re-reading the lines of the Chinese poet Li Tai Po in Alfred Meyer's English translation. I became absorbed by his poetical metaphysics. The poems, filled with simplicity and wisdom, are about the solitude of man, about the transience of youthful beauty and the inevitability of death. MacMillan had been thinking about this ballet for many years, and when he started choreographing it, achieved an elaborate precision and depth that succeeded in expressing the ideas of Mahler and Li Tai Po in the language of dance.

The neo-classical language of *The Song of the Earth* is complicated. It demands exceptional stamina and deep emotional involvement. For me it became comfortable at once, because my emotional response to the music automatically made my body assume the only possible attitude the choreographer could have found, and that left me the possibility of individual accents in each movement.

With Anthony Dowell

The rich metaphysical content of the ballet was translated by MacMillan into a vague plot about two lovers who are separated by death, following the implacable laws of nature, and who are reunited in death at the end of the ballet.

Metaphysical themes are familiar to me. When I dance in ballets with a plot—*Giselle* or *Swan Lake* or *Manon*—I always try to interpret these themes in the language of dance, within the context of the ballet's general idea, so that a particular case becomes a manifestation of an eternal law. In *The Song of the Earth,* I was confronted with an opposite task: to find an individual interpretation of the ballet's abstract notions, and to reach the inner state of mind necessary for me to feel comfortable in any role; to sense the theme physically and filter it through my body. I simply refused to dance the general idea that all living things are doomed to death. I believe that life, with its renewal, is never conquered. This is expressed in the last lines of the cycle:

The lovely earth, all, everywhere,

Revives in spring and blooms anew,

All, everywhere and ever, ever

Shines the blue horizon,

ever . . . ever . . .

In Mahler's music one doesn't hear death itself, but rather the German concept of *der Ewige,* "the eternal." This notion does imply a constant threat of death, or rather a continual reminder of our inevitable death, a memento mori. In MacMillan's ballet the idea is personified in the figure of a stranger who constantly emerges from among the abstract characters wearing a mask that helps distinguish him from the others.

I danced in the second part ("The Lonely One in Autumn") and in the fifth part ("Farewell"). If, in the first part, "The Drinking Song of Earthly Woe," we hear the theme of "The Feast During the Plague," the enjoyment of earthly delights before death strikes, the second part is filled with a premonition, lived through in the solitude of this fatal hour, with all its knowledge of the inevitability of coming death. I decided to fill my movement with the idea of human will—yes, I am the last leaf remaining on the tree struck by the autumn winds, I will soon be torn off and flung into nothingness, I am doomed, I know it, and yet I cannot fully believe it. Just as a convict waiting to be shot at dawn, or a patient with terminal cancer, cannot accept, even at his last breath, the physical reality of death, I do not believe until the very last moment that my life will be terminated. I came on stage with all the knowledge of my imminent death, but also with a last spark of hope that prevailed to the very moment of death. This was my personal response to the theme, the music, and the choreography.

Of course, the choreography allowed other interpretations—its emotional amplitude did not place any rigid limits on the dancer's imagination. In my case, this feeling—"I know I am doomed, I live with this knowledge, but I still hope to survive"—helped me to find the link between the second and the fifth parts. In "Farewell," with my dead lover I went into death, into eternity, accompanied by *der Ewige*. I had accepted my doom, I was no longer afraid of death, I was no longer struggling, and I felt no bitterness. I felt an almost Buddhist serenity in my soul, as if I were on the threshold of transfiguration to the heights of pure spirit. This serenity could be conveyed to the audience only by overcoming the physical strain of the muscles. Like the Red soldiers in Yakobson's *The Twelve,* I went in slow motion into eternity, flooded by a growing light, as if letting eternity pass through my body. I did not have to act anything. I had only to listen to the music and the incessant whisper of death calling to me, to my subconscious. It was the call of death and at the same time a subconscious death wish. I had to make my every movement reveal to the spectators that nothing else existed for me. I heard death, I was facing it, I was accepting it.

The final outburst of resistance was staged remarkably by MacMillan in the driving bourrées that began at the footlights and then crossed the stage diagonally. At the end of the diagonal my lover embraced me, and this embrace symbolized our reunion in death. These bourrées demand enormous stamina—and in the finale, when a dancer is absolutely exhausted. For me they were even more exhausting because of the efforts I was making to reach an equilibrium between the physical strain and the feeling of serene grace I must have in meeting death. The driving propulsion of these bourrées is reminiscent of a leaf carried away by a gust of wind, a continuation of the metaphor from the second part. The ballet was originally staged for Marcia Haydée, who has a very strong pointe, and who was said to be overwhelming in this sequence. I have never had a good pointe, and there was not one rehearsal where I could dance the bourrées correctly. At the dress rehearsal I concentrated all my strength on them, and when it was over, the dancers standing around started applauding me. It was incredibly satisfying, for nothing is more important to me than impartial recognition by my colleagues.

The Song of the Earth confirmed my real connection with the Royal Ballet. With Tudor's *Dark Elegies,* I had added another Mahler ballet to my experience. I wish I could dance to Mahler once again, but it must be a ballet with the highest metaphysical level of choreographic images, so that it can challenge and mobilize all my inner resources, as happened with MacMillan's choreography. I think *The Song of the Earth* remains his best work.

I first saw *Manon* during an engagement of the Royal Ballet in New York, with Antoinette Sibley and Anthony Dowell, both of whom I liked—

but I liked the role of Manon even more. Probably no other of my roles in the West means as much to me as Manon—and not only because I've loved l'Abbé Prévost's novel from childhood (though I've never re-read it as an adult). Manon's very character I see as one of the most enchanting and complex in French literature. She has been turned into a symbol of feminine inconsistency, perfidy, flippancy: "Butterfly, thou art all inconsistency . . . colorful and unfaithful pharaoh." To me, this is a superficial view of her.

Although she is what the French call *une putain respectueuse*, for me Manon's uniqueness lies in her existential nature. She sees her own life apart from the mass of humanity, apart from society's moral prohibitions, and she lives without a backward glance. She lives according to the feminine dictates of her instinct, her will, her caprice; all the facets of the feminine character are vividly reflected in her. She is fickle, yet, in a way, consistent in her attractions. Greedy and generous, unhappy with the restlessness and changeability of her feelings and happy with them too, she is both superficial and deep. Manon feels the excitement of a life that provokes her, as if she were a gambler, to all kinds of madness. Like a butterfly, she lives for the moment, extracting from it all the excitement she can. Unashamed and bound by only one law—that there is no tomorrow—she gives herself over to today's passion. At the same time she fully knows that the day will come when she must pay the price. The Shakespearean "Tis better to be vile than vile esteem'd" is applicable to her. And she is ready to pay for her passions, for the pleasure of living fully, for not being satisfied with pale compromises or imitations. In life, one has to pay for everything anyway, so far better to pay for something real! An aura of excitement hovers even over her death—des Grieux digs her grave with his spurs, and in this I see a sort of chivalrous tribute to love from Manon's creator to his enchanting heroine.

MacMillan's choreography is very effective in the pas de deux. Because there is no strict structure in MacMillan's choreography, only an outline and the general contours, it is full of places where each performer can fill it out as she wishes, in accordance with her own individuality. It is no accident that all five Manons at Covent Garden—Sibley, Lynn Seymour, and the others—are utterly individual. Some emphasize Manon's greed, others her frivolity, but every one is convincing. This role touches (and gives great satisfaction to) the theatrical nerve in any ballerina.

At the first rehearsal I took to Manon at once, as many years before at the Kirov I had taken to Giselle. I sensed the same joyous feeling of extraordinary freedom which makes it possible to slip into a role as into a custom-made dress that fits perfectly. Then, at rehearsal, it is not necessary to consider the purely physical movement (how to sit, look, stand); you can rely on improvisation. I was sure that Manon would not let me down, because I count on the rehearsed feeling of control and even forget about it

Rehearsing CONCERTO *with Ivan Nagy*

for a moment in order to live the role. This feeling of true life, of the naturalness of what is being experienced within the conditions set forth, was born immediately. And at the dress rehearsal it was confirmed: it was November 21, my birthday, and when Manon, in exile, leaves the ship in the last act, I felt myself so much inside her skin that I did not at first react to the unfamiliar music the orchestra suddenly started playing. I was just beginning to lament the fact that I still didn't know the music sufficiently well, when I noticed all my colleagues smiling and realized that the orchestra was playing "Happy Birthday."

At the premiere, my presentiments did not deceive me: I felt so accustomed to the action of the ballet that I almost forgot about the audience. I recall how, in the first act, I sat on my chair in a relaxed pose and watched des Grieux—Anthony Dowell—performing a variation with exceptional purity. "You were looking at me with such excitement," he said after the performance. I actually hadn't been aware of that; I had simply been taking pleasure in his dancing and perceiving it as part of life rather than as a convention of the ballet.

With *Manon*, close artistic contact sprang up between me and Dowell. When we were first partners in *Giselle*, we had no feeling for each other. But the more I worked with him, the more I became enchanted with his inherent gentlemanliness, his tact, the great emotional support he always gives. After *Manon*, I was convinced that he felt genuine interest in my work, that he looked forward to something spontaneous and complicated from me to which he could respond with the sincerity natural to him. He is unusually sensitive to any falsity on stage and responds only to natural emotions—and that is equally important to me in performance. For me, being a partner is a kind of human speech, and it inspires me only when there is mutual human interest between the speakers. I came constantly to feel this interest in Dowell. Working together enriched us both. It took time for him to understand that, physically, the duel ought to be light and unconstrained. He did not permit me to fall into the slightest affectation, to which he would have been extremely sensitive, and, as a result, I felt myself unusually free with him. And at the same time I took pleasure in the control which Anthony possesses to the highest degree.

In this way, *Manon* with Dowell transformed my Giselle in England. Our best performance was in Battersea Park, although the atmosphere was highly inappropriate for ballet. We danced in a tent as in the circus, and the staging there did not inspire any particular enthusiasm in me. Nonetheless, we were both in a special mood. In the audience and within us there was such silence and peace that I felt an unusual fullness in every gesture. And, within the framework of the performance, this fullness did not diminish but continued to flow on like a river carrying me along in its current. I did not have to act; I simply lived my life on stage and took pleasure in my freedom and naturalness, as Manon had always taken pleasure in hers.

Various ballets set different tasks for you: *Manon,* for instance, draws you into a circle of particularly dramatic problems, because the choreography itself is not sufficiently expressive. Balanchine means, first of all, the solution of stylistic problems. So does Bronislava Nijinska's ballet *Les Biches,* which she staged in the twenties for Diaghilev and, later, revived for the Royal Ballet. I was intrigued by this ballet, its unusually difficult and aesthetic choreography, its atmosphere woven out of reserve and veiled, subtly executed eroticism that unites the participants in a fashionable party—three girls in pink and three athletic youths from the beach.

I danced the most puzzling figure, *la garçonne,* the girl in a blue tunic who embodies sexual ambivalence. My heroine gave rise to a good deal of discussion. Some said she was typically AC / DC, others that she was basically asexual. . . . Having thought about it, I decided to take Marlene Dietrich as my model. Her androgynous nature had always interested me, and it was terribly absorbing to create on stage a type of beauty that has already passed away—the type of the twenties.

The summer of 1974 was full of feverish tension for me. I was swamped with new works for the Royal, and on July 3 my *Bayadère* was scheduled to be baptized in New York, the mere thought of which made me break out in a cold sweat. Then, on June 30, at 5 a.m., the telephone rang in my London apartment: it was Mischa Baryshnikov calling from Toronto, where he was on tour with the Kirov. In a trembling voice, stammering and upset, he told me he had taken a firm decision to remain in the West and had already asked for political asylum in Canada. Of course, I tried to reassure him in every way and promised to do all that I could for him at ABT—I was flying to New York the next day.

I realized that for a dancer like Mischa, ABT was the only place in America where he could immediately display his phenomenal technique and artistry. ABT was the only company that had the classical repertory he was familiar with, such as *Giselle,* the *Don Quixote* pas de deux, and now my "Shades" from *La Bayadère.* As soon as I arrived in New York, I phoned Lucia Chase (she had heard about Mischa, but had never seen him) and described his situation to her. I said I wanted to dance a few performances with him—there would be no other chance for him to dance in New York that summer. Although I was scheduled to dance *Giselle* with Ivan Nagy, I hoped he would understand that this was a true emergency. Soon everything was arranged, and Mischa arrived in New York in the second half of July.

Our reunion was filled with emotion; we had not seen each other for four years. He had remained in my memory as a very young and very talented dancer who, when I had seen him last, had had little partnering experience. At our first rehearsal in New York I was pleasantly surprised to find in him a remarkable partner and a mature artist.

Now, when I look back at the years we have spent in the West, I can see the invisible threads that linked us, the three fugitives from the Kirov, together. In 1961 I danced my first *Giselle* in London, thanks to the unexpected flight of Nureyev; this performance made me known in the West, and it happened to be the beginning of my attachment to London and the Royal Ballet. In 1970 my first performance after my own defection was with Rudi, on BBC television. And then in 1974, as if guided by a premonition, I timed the premiere of the "Shades" to Mischa's defection, and danced with him *Giselle* and the pas de deux from *Don Quixote* in New York, the center of the ballet world, where he could at once display all his qualities in the most favorable light.

Our first *Giselle*, on July 27, was a triumph; Baryshnikov took New York by storm. On that evening I was dancing for him. I remembered how important it had been for me to have such psychological support from Ivan and Erik in my own first weeks in America, and I tried to do for Mischa what they had done for me.

We have danced a great deal together since. Dancing with Mischa is different for me from any other partnership; only with him do I feel as if there were an electrically charged field around me, and a unique atmosphere of constructive rivalry and competition, as if we charge each other with voltage. We have a common school behind us; we have common aesthetic principles and a complete mutual understanding. When I dance with him, I feel as if I were shielded by this common strength, and probably just because of that at our rehearsals we often fool around, bicker a little, and in general never behave very seriously, as if we were preserving our strength for the performance. The rehearsals are just a warm-up.

And yet in January of 1977, after almost a year's interval, we were able to dance *Giselle* without a single rehearsal, when Mischa replaced Ivan, who had injured himself two hours before the beginning of the performance. Now our artistic paths cross less often: Mischa danced primarily with ABT, while I divided my time between ABT and the Royal. His decision to join Balanchine's company made the prospects of our partnership even more remote. I understood and accepted his decision, as any artist understands a colleague who cannot bear routine and monotony in his artistic career. For Mischa, Balanchine's ballets are *terra incognita:* they imply a totally new dancing vocabulary, and he wants his perceptive body to master it. I am happy for him. We have somewhat different aesthetic criteria; he is much more artistically promiscuous than I am. In the eight years in which I have tried all the styles, I have danced in a lot of trashy pieces which, in their own way, were helpful to me in my "Western" career. Now I have in a way restricted myself; I have become more selective. Today I do not want to spend my time on things not in line with my own ideas of our art.

I recall one argument with Mischa about a ballet he wanted me to do. I refused: the ballet seemed totally uninteresting to me. Then he reproached me by saying that a dancer cannot give his entire life to *Giselle* and *Swan Lake*. But I am sure that one can, because the old classical ballets are like classical literature; after a certain time one re-reads them differently. They are a check on one's human maturity, experience, attitude to the world and to life. I will never tire of dancing the classics, because I keep changing all the time, like any human being. I "die and resurrect under a new persona," and my Giselle, Odette, Sylphide, and Aurora change with me. Each time I bring something new to my interpretations, new touches, fresh nuances that depend on the level of my human maturity in general, and on my mood of the day in particular. My fidelity to the classics does not imply a rejection of experimentation, however. I am ready to experiment and to take risks—but only on condition that the experiment has a meaning, a content that will justify the physical and emotional strain involved. To waste my time on trifles, even if they are chic or ultra-modern by current fashion, is out of the question for me. It is against my taste and against my artistic experience.

I think Jerome Robbins' *Other Dances* is the most successful work Mischa and I did together. This ballet was connected with Jerry's earlier *Dances at a Gathering*, which I was to dance in London later in 1976. *Other Dances* was staged by Jerry especially for the two of us, and probably because of this, our contact with him was deeper than with other choreographers whose work we performed. I had the luck of getting to know him better on a personal level, and it helped me to master his unique style. If I were to define the basic feature of Jerry's choreography, I would say it was an innate sense of movement that is always strictly and rationally controlled. There are rational choreographers' whose creations are calculated; there are those whose work is born out of feelings filtered through the body. Jerry belongs to the latter category, but he has a very precise logical mastery over the emotion. His method of thinking is choreographic: music passing through his mind transforms itself into precise choreographic combinations. These definitive plastic forms of expression do not come at once; before he makes one final choice, he tries thousands of variants and accents. But his final choice is always at one with the music and with the dancer's body. I feel comfortable and happy in his ballets because of his clear vision of what he wants me to do. The natural response of my body to the music and the movements dictated by Jerry are in complete harmony. It is always natural for me to live within his creative system.

Jerry, whose own career as a dancer gave him special insights, never exploits a dancer's body, he never tries to squeeze it into a preconceived scheme or to impose anything on it. He senses you as an individual dancer, and he gives you the possibility of finding the organic nature of the movement. I have never even thought of changing anything in Jerry's compositions. To me they are built in the only conceivable way. His chore-

With Mikhail Baryshnikov

ography never tends to lace the body into a corset; on the contrary, there is always, between the body and his choreographic design, a "clearance" that guarantees the necessary freedom to develop nuances and stylistic colorings. In *Other Dances* the body seems to be weaving a shawl of Valenciennes lace; the choreographic design is the fabric of the lace, and the space between the threads is filled with the pauses, the hesitations, the subtle nuances, that fine understatement of movement that for me is the most precious feature of the romantic—and, for that matter, of any— ballet. For me, Jerry Robbins is the most romantic of all the neo-classical choreographers.

On the surface he is like Balanchine, working primarily in the genre of the plotless ballet, but the degree of abstraction is not as great with Robbins. He is less geometric and for me he is more poetic, because in his choreography there is always room for self-expression. I do not feel I am a mere instrument following precisely the prescribed design. Besides, though Jerry's ballets do not have traditional plots, they always have something reminiscent of one, which is hard to articulate in a logical way. When I perform *Other Dances* with Mischa, we always try to convey a certain dramatic message to the audience. This message cannot be put into a few words, like "he loves her, and she does not respond" or vice versa. The message lies, rather, in Jerry's lyrical variations to the music of Chopin, full of poetic subtleties that remain unspoken.

While watching Jerry's works—*Dances at a Gathering,* which is for me an existential ballet about "individual solitudes," to use the words of Rilke, or the more rational *Goldberg Variations*—it may seem there is no "modern" innovation in their choreography; Jerry does not oversaturate his neo-classics with modern dance. The strength of his choreography lies in its natural expressive means, which are subordinate not only to the structure but to the very spirit of the music. In this respect, as an interpreter of Chopin, he is unique. *Other Dances* may be the most obvious proof of it: here Jerry accentuates the gracefulness, humor, and lyrical warmth of Chopin's music. The Polish touch in the stylized cracovienne steps skillfully and inconspicuously decorates intricate neo-classical supports and arabesques, creating a precise Slavic coloration.

When I ask him what I should do in this or that piece, he often answers: "You yourself know best." But when he does give me advice, he always hits the mark. When I rehearsed the last variation to the mazurka in *Other Dances*, Jerry said, "Imagine that you are Isadora on pointe." And freedom of movement came at once. Yet as a dramatic actress I cannot realize myself to the full in the refined miniature world of Robbins. I dream of a full-length ballet Jerry might do for me one day. It could be a ballet of any genre—drama, comedy, even farce—that would put acting possibilities before me, that would have human characters and a dramatic plot. In recent years, I have found this only in *Manon.*

Among the neo-classical ballets I have danced in recent years, Glen Tetley's *Voluntaries* was for me no less an experience than *The Song of the Earth*. I danced it for the first time in London in November 1976, and it has given me great joy to dance it ever since.

Tetley dedicated this ballet to the memory of John Cranko, a talented choreographer and true artist. But *Voluntaries* is not an elegiac reflection on Cranko's sudden death or on death in general; not a pietà, invoking sorrow and compassion. In it, rather, Tetley grasps the essence of Poulenc's music and finds a convincing dance equivalent to it. The music—the solemn bursts of an organ Mass ascending to the spires of a Gothic cathedral—is filled with a rigorous creative impulse: sentimental contemplation or graceful sorrow is alien to it. One can feel in it a strongly masculine attitude toward the very idea of death: the idea of overcoming sorrow, of conquering death, by a concentration of inner energy straining for the creation that will survive its creator, for death has no power over such achievement.

Voluntaries does not have any plot (the title is taken from the musical term referring to free improvisations by the trumpet or organ before, during, and after a Catholic Mass), but the choreographic structure of the ballet is extremely meaningful to me. The whole work is built by Tetley on one pose: a resilient cross of the outstretched arms with the belly drawn in and the head thrown back in a position imitating the Crucifixion.

When I was rehearsing this ballet with Tetley, he wanted me to perform this and a few related movements as if overcoming the utmost muscle strain, overcoming myself, through pain and torment (Christ's torment, as if breaking some inner chains that were holding me). It was a clue to the enormous inner intensity of the ballet, so rare in modern neo-classics, and I felt it immediately. It was also a clue to the plastic of *Voluntaries* that became mine from the first rehearsal. I found the necessary physical strain; I learned to induce that state of mind when the soul is hovering on the brink of despair and yet never gives in to despair. It is a triumph of such inner strength that proves the unlimited capacities of the human body and soul to endure pain and suffering and, finally, to overcome them. Even death, symbolized by the Crucifixion, can be overcome by physical resistance and an almost unbearable strain: first by abandoning oneself to that strain, relaxing in that resistance, and then by triumphing in the final resurrection.

The style of *Voluntaries* is incompatible with the use of expressively "empty" arms, arms that don't feel the stretching of their sinews and muscles, and arms that fail to perfectly combine the tense angularity of their movements with their cantilena-like flow in the pas de deux. I respond to this combination and feel comfortable in such choreography: the body overcoming its own resistance, fighting its way through inner torment to resurrection, to creation (one can suggest many other interpretations), becomes a rich plastic metaphor in itself. Essentially, the ballet is a paraphrase of the Biblical "death, by death subdued," conceived in a very masculine manner.

Voluntaries is difficult to dance, because its choreography demands an extreme concentration in order to show the inner strain that lies so close to despair. Every time I dance this ballet I try to work myself into an inner state born from a variety of feelings but always based on my conception of the ballet: resurrection through the act of creation. Each time I rationalize this state in a different way, in different words—"Learn to live alone, learn to overcome anything," or, "Have faith and live by faith"—and each time I must do this to develop that deep concentration without which it is impossible to fill with profound meaning the angular movements designed by Tetley and to render them with the utmost flexibility of the body.

In Glen's *Le Sacre du Printemps,* I found myself in a quite different world that was more formalistic and mechanical. I undertook *Le Sacre* because I had never worked on this kind of modern choreography before, and was primarily concerned with extending my ballet vocabulary.

Sacre's steps are exceedingly difficult, especially the contractions, and they are unusual for any classical dancer. It is a big technical challenge for the body to switch from pure academic patterns to the ultra-modern elements which dominate *Le Sacre.* I can easily change from *Swan Lake* to *Voluntaries,* but the transition from *Le Sacre* to *Sleeping Beauty* is almost painful. What is more, this kind of modern ballet may either jeopardize one's ability to perform the classics properly or extend the physical possibilities of a classically trained body; it may enlarge the extension and flexibility of muscles by giving them additional freedom. I danced both *Sacre* and *Sleeping Beauty* during the spring season at ABT, and remember the tremendous effort it cost me.

As I have said, I seldom danced *Sleeping Beauty* in Russia, and had worked very little on this ballet. In Leningrad I usually danced Florine—this role became mine at once. Somehow I immediately understood her French elegance and the filigree quality of her movement, though when I danced it for the first time, I was only a senior student in the ballet school. In our graduation performance I danced the Blue Bird pas de deux with Yuri Soloviev.

So it was in the West that I saw this ballet for the first time as an immense technical challenge and decided to assimilate its style.

Stylistically *The Sleeping Beauty* is more complicated than *Swan Lake,* which nevertheless remains for me the most difficult ballet, draining all my physical and emotional strength. *Sleeping Beauty* is a kind of encyclopedia of academic dance: the purity of the positions, ideal turn-out, balance, and faultless positioning of hands and arms are the decisive elements. Without this crystalline purity one can never master the elegant, refined, and exquisite style of the ballet. Its choreography glitters with all the colors of the spectrum of the mature Petipa's art.

arsing OTHER DANCES *with Jerome Robbins and Mikhail Baryshnikov*

As far as the plastic vocabulary of *The Sleeping Beauty* is concerned, more than any other ballet it approaches the pure academic dance class at its fullest extent.

In *The Sleeping Beauty* you cannot improvise with your arms and hands as you can in *Swan Lake,* where the arms are the wings, struggling, flapping, a visual metaphor of Odette's confusion and torment. In *The Sleeping Beauty* all the positions of the arms are strict and formal, and the positions of the feet are a stylized imitation of the positions of the ladies at the court of the Sun King, holding their dresses out over their hoops. This extends through the entire ballet and it must be faultless, just as all the fifth positions must be completely closed. *Sleeping Beauty* allows no imprecision, no sloppiness that may endanger its style. All Aurora's variations, technically complex as they are, must be performed with ease, with no visible strain, so that the audience can never guess how much effort a dancer makes to perform all these intricate combinations. Otherwise there will be no sixteen-year-old girl named Aurora (the Dawn) enjoying her serene youth.

To master this technique once and forever, so that the body always performs it automatically, never digressing from the classical canon, was particularly difficult for me. Each time I had to fight my impetuous nature, those impulses and abrupt changes in mood on which I depend so much on stage. I had to subdue my hyper-emotional nature to the strict and rigid choreographic design, to lace myself within it. I had to avoid two other traps hidden in this ballet: I did not want to turn this refined style into affected mannerism or to replace the inspired dance by academic classwork.

The ideal model of Aurora for me had always been Margot Fonteyn, with her faultless taste in performing Petipa's most filigree vignettes and her remarkable musicality and the charm of everlasting youth that radiated from her. The best Aurora I saw in Russia was Irina Kolpakova, whose dancing was a triumph of perfect academism, although she lacked the charm of femininity. Her Aurora looked too much like a doll, it was sexless, unlike Fonteyn's, and I am sure that Aurora must have this touch of femininity about her—it is a necessary seasoning for her.

Compared to *Swan Lake, The Sleeping Beauty* is more difficult in yet another aspect: the purity of its style is a *sine qua non* of its expressivity. In *Swan Lake* expressive acting may partially cover the technical or stylistic imperfections of a dancer: good acting will make them go unnoticed by the public. That is impossible in *The Sleeping Beauty.* Strictly speaking, there is no material for acting in it: it is an allegory of spring, of first love, of the eternal renaissance of life, and like any allegory it is a little dry. The impact of *The Sleeping Beauty* is rooted in its faultless stylistic charm, which is based on the perfection of academic dancing. Its expressivity comes from the image of Aurora—the charm of her youth not yet familiar with the hardships of life, serene and natural as breathing.

But it is in my nature to respond more to any manifestation of discordance or dramatic conflict (the conflict in *Sleeping Beauty* is very symbolic: the eternal fight between good and evil in a most general form) than to a heavenly purity, and so it was a hard task for me to find the necessary seraphic serenity. My Russian experience taught me that if I do not find this state of mind, I can easily fall into the affectation characteristic of my first experiments with Aurora. Probably that was the reason why the more stylized Florine was so easy for me to dance. Of course, the lucky combination of elegance and bravura in Florine was also very helpful: I never had to harness my own emotions (in general, I have never had any difficulties with bravura). The refinement of Aurora must be simple but never common. It is a special aristocratic simplicity in manner so remarkably characteristic of Margot Fonteyn both on the stage and in everyday life.

In the course of the ballet the character of Aurora's refinement changes slightly: in the third act the manner of the princess who has slept for a century acquires a touch of triumph, which is understandable: she's been awakened by a kiss, she is a bride, she is on the threshold of a new life.

I had a hard time with all the technical difficulties, and I could not find the necessary youthful state of mind. As usual, a lucky chance helped me. In Maggie Black's school, where I was then taking class, there was a girl student who, I discovered later, was an admirer of my dancing. I noticed her at once, not only because of her natural physical qualities but also because I felt immediately that she had an intense spiritual life, a certain freedom in her movements, both dignity and charm. When Maggie introduced her to me, my first impression was confirmed. Of course, the girl was shy, but the dignity and natural freedom of her plasticity passed on to me. I found the essence of my Aurora. I felt my shoulders relaxing; my body and neck lost their strain.

And my third *Sleeping Beauty* brought me satisfaction.

The Song of the Earth and *Voluntaries* are probably the best extended works from the neo-classical repertoire that I have danced in recent years. I would also include *Romeo and Juliet,* the very same ballet of Igor Tchernishov's which was killed on the spot at the Kirov and to which I gave life on American soil in April of 1977. The idea of reviving Igor's cancelled work was that of his ex-wife, Elena Kittel-Tchernishova, who had emigrated from Russia and was working at the time with the Maryland Ballet. I have always been very sympathetic to the artistic director there, Kathleen Crofton, and respect her knowledge of the Russian school, her taste, and her high standards. So it was with very little hesitation that I accepted Elena's offer to perform in Baltimore. In this I saw a certain psychological revenge—to realize in America that which had been rejected in Russia. I was not without doubts as to whether Igor's choreography, which had once seemed like

Rehearsing ROMEO AND JULIET. *Top: With Ivan Nagy. Bottom: With Elena Tchernishova*

such a revelation, had not aged in the intervening eight years. However, in this experiment there was a unique challenge, and my curiosity could not resist.

Elena had initiated the production in Russia. She had assisted Igor, and now, years later, she undertook to resurrect the choreography of a ballet which had been performed on stage only once. It was not at all easy for her, as it had not been for me with *La Bayadère,* but in the course of several months she reconstructed the performance as a whole from bits and pieces, while herself supplying certain linkages and small details in accordance with Tchernishov's style.

The dancers for the main parts were gathered haphazardly—Romeo was Ivan Nagy; Mercutio, Helgi Tomasson from Balanchine's company; Tybalt, a soloist from the Maryland Ballet, Sylvester Campbell. There was no time to spare—I was up to my neck in my performances with ABT at Washington's Kennedy Center, to which Elena would travel from rehearsing the corps de ballet in Baltimore in order to work with me. Ivan was on tour somewhere. Helgi could find time for only a few rehearsals. Only Sylvester was more or less available. Elena worked out individual bits with everybody, in the best Hollywood tradition. And the dress rehearsal was essentially the first time we mounted the entire ballet (the matinee on April 17 functioned as the true dress rehearsal). When we all came out on stage together, the Shakespearean arch-enemies, Mercutio-Helgi and Tybalt-Sylvester, gazed at one another for the first time with a pleasant look of surprise and sympathy.

We worked at a breakneck speed such as I had never before experienced, not even in the West. The day before the premiere, our very badly sewn costumes were redone, and the quite inappropriate sets were tossed out. Elena replaced them artfully with dark green cloth in front of which the only adornment was provided by copper lanterns which hinted at the Capulets' ball and created a generalized poetic atmosphere.

At the matinee, Ivan and I were trembling, and things got confusing. In the adagio Ivan forgot the order and went into an improvisation which we barely managed to get out of. But the evening performance went off quite properly, although I did feel I was not entirely inside the role. That freedom which is absolutely necessary to me was missing. But I was satisfied with my experiment with Ivan, who turned out to be truly effective as Romeo, and it seemed to me that the choreography had not lost its expressiveness; both the seventeen-minute adagio, which Elena compressed to thirteen minutes, and the deaths of Romeo and Juliet were as dramatic as they had been in Leningrad, filled with the special passion characteristic of Tchernishov.

This was my fourth Juliet—different from MacMillan's psychological one, Tudor's aesthetic stylization, Lavrovsky's pedestrian girl. This was actually not a Shakespearean Juliet at all, but one taken from the romantic legend about the immortal lovers and brought up to contemporary times and somewhat abstracted. But this abstraction, however expressive, was no longer entirely satisfying to me—I wanted a richer role which would have permitted me, as with my Manon, to live it and dance it. I really felt this richness only in Juliet's "insane" monologue before her death, which brought back to me the best dramatic moments in Yakobson's ballets. Yet surely this ballet is worth returning to in the future.

I am writing this last chapter at my home in San Francisco, awaiting the birth of my child. I danced my last performance in August 1977, and now for the first time in my not very long, but one might say extensive, career in the ballet I am experiencing the bliss of leisure. From the windows of my house, there is a view of the water and the mountains which reminds me of the Crimea—actually, it is Sausalito beyond the famous Golden Gate Bridge. On the broad lawn stretching from the Bay to Marina Boulevard, people are walking their dogs or are out with their children or doing their morning jogging. A peaceful life, in which I do not take part, goes on. I toss a fur coat on my shoulders and walk back and forth in my tiny garden, ten paces up and back. I have temporarily cut myself off from the external world and concentrate entirely on myself, on my thoughts, on the books I am consuming in great quantities, and on my own book. And I have again started to paint (for the second time in my life in the West). Earlier, during my first years in America, I painted because it was an emotional outlet for me, a soothing release. Now, I'm painting in order to give my fantasies an outlet, for my own satisfaction, dilettantishly taking joy in the fact that out of a confusing mix of colors the contours of what was only an hour ago a hazy idea or intention is breaking through on canvas.

I paint and I think. And most often I think about my future child, of course. I am having it in the middle of my career, and I think: Almost none of the major ballerinas of this century had children. Pavlova, Fonteyn, Spessivtseva, Ulanova, Plisetskaya. . . . I wonder why? Was that pure egoism? Or a sacrifice they were obliged to offer to the stage, which demanded it like a pagan god? The tribute paid for total absorption in the ballet, for that unbelievable joy which it can give so generously? Or fear of losing one's form after giving birth, of losing the extension, the suppleness of the back, the shape of the feet, which could become deformed? And what if that happened to me? Could I live without the stage? I absolutely couldn't dance in bad shape, and at one stroke, wipe out everything good that I have tried to accomplish. For me, there is nothing worse than to defile the ballet by performing badly that which depends not only on a divine spark but on form as well.

The ballet . . . what essentially is this thankless art? In the dramatic theatre, the film, in the fine arts, in writing, it is possible to rest for half a year and then return and begin to create something new. But consider Marina Semyonova, who after the birth of her daughter was never able to recover her form. Tragically and slavishly we depend upon the body, upon its physical habits and caprices; we wear it out to our last ounce of strength. And our masochistic labor is wiped away like marks in the sand, and years of grinding effort—all of that single combat with the body at rehearsal and in performance—pass away into nothing, as if they had never been. Is the ballet worth such sacrifice? I don't know the answer.

I paint, bending over the easel. I paint my Madonnas, my Leda and the Swan, and think: This canvas will remain, even my amateur canvas, which is important only to me. Certainly a professional artist's canvas remains. And he imprints on it his internal experience, his relationship to life—illuminations which may be fixed or stopped in color. But what remains of our art? Of our illuminations? They are momentary, alive for only one evening; they remain only in the memory of those who were present. And even that impression is frail and changeable: the farther away it goes, the more unfaithful it becomes and the more tinged by memory, and the more difficult it becomes to remember *what* it really was and *how* it was. I know exactly what it is on stage to let go of my control and improvise, still supported by that control. Suddenly new details come, precisely and expressively—but I myself cannot remember them. Perhaps they remain in the memory of others.

Will the ballet take second place to my child? Will the responsibility for its life break my attachment to the stage? And how will I be able to coordinate my endless travelling from city to city and from country to country with my child's daily need of me and my need for it? Or can I possibly live completely without the ballet?

During these years, I have danced all the classical ballets; I have tested myself in the neo-classics, in modern dance, in jazz. I have danced things by almost all the major choreographers other than Martha Graham and Roland Petit. Probably I could stop now, since I do not see any interesting new ballets coming along, even in the distant future. And to subsist day by day on the usual stuff of which I have danced a great deal in my eight years in the West, things I have not even mentioned in this book, is not worth it; my perfectionism has grown stronger and I have become even more demanding of myself. But that is not the main thing. If I come back in good form and dance only my unfailing *Giselle* and *Swan Lake* and nothing essentially new in the coming years, will I be able to uncover something new within me, something neither I nor the public now know?

I think so. I can respond positively to the question I constantly ask myself—is the ballet worth such effort? It is, if you are a perfectionist and if every performance is an examination—a test of that internal experience which is the thing of value that has remained with me through all these

years, the thing that is inextricably bound up with my self. We all pass
through definite cycles in the course of which we die and are reborn, and
at each new turn of the spiral we return to life renewed. Now, I feel that
one of these cycles has come round, and that my internal experience in *Giselle* and *Swan Lake* will make itself felt differently. So there will be no
repetition.

With the years, I have grown more understanding, much more tolerant; I
have learned to distinguish the important from the insignificant, to grasp
the essence. In many ways, this book has helped me. Working on it and
putting into words what has lived an almost unconscious life within me, I
understand more precisely all I have done and all I still want to do in the
ballet. I once said in an interview that I dance for myself and for at least
one other person in the hall. I have been writing this book for myself and
for one other person, the ideal reader to whom my considerations will seem
interesting.

And this book is the answer to my second question: Can I live without
the ballet?

I can imagine myself not being on stage—but I cannot imagine existing
outside art. Yet it is difficult to believe that there will be no more rehearsals, no more feverish agitation before performances; that there will be
something else instead. I have done much, but strangely, no feeling of
peace follows from that. And it seems to me at this moment that I have
simply sat down for a rest, in expectation of something new.

EPILOGUE

This pause did not last very long. On February 1, 1978, in the hospital affiliated with the University of California, Makarova gave birth to her first child, named in honor of her two favorite Apostles, André-Michel. Three and a half months later, on May 10, Makarova was brilliantly dancing Jerome Robbins' *Other Dances* at the Met, partnered by Mikhail Baryshnikov. These are the bare facts, but behind them are hidden hours and days crammed with practicing, filled with triumphs, defeats, despair, even tears. These three and a half months, devoted exclusively to restoring Makarova's balletic shape (although for her first month she also nursed her son), became one of the most intense periods in her life. Her existence assumed such a crazy, breakneck pace that she simply had no time to examine the metamorphosis that was taking place within her. This process has not yet become her past, and that is why she refused to write the final pages of this book. "I still don't realize how I managed to get back into shape so fast, considering what kind of body I had to deal with."

"Who rides the tiger can never get off," says the Chinese proverb. In Makarova's case this tiger has been her rebellious body, whose unpredictable reactions and whims she has been accustomed to fighting since her early days at the Kirov. It is amusing to listen to Makarova speak about her body, relating to it as a kind of perfidious ally or persistent enemy. She has referred to her recent duel with her body as a joyous combat of the two wills. "At the outset everything worked for me. My body seemed not to resist too much; it gave in. Suddenly my leg rose on its own. I wasn't able to jump at all, and then out of the blue I started jumping so high I couldn't believe my eyes!"

As a witness to this peculiar "taming of the shrew" I should report that the struggle was uneven and painful. And if Makarova considered her swift return to good shape a miracle, the miracle was her persistence and hard work. It was a miracle of her will, of tremendous effort exerted over weakened muscles that, having been liberated from their years of imposed training, were now enjoying untrammeled freedom. With all the vehemence and passion in her nature, Makarova involved herself in this combat with her body, whose muscles did not obey her control, behaving as if they had a life of their own. How many times at rehearsals did she look desperately at her disobedient legs and exclaim, "What am I supposed to do with them? They're going wherever they want to!"

She began this struggle instantly, the day after André's birth. As she merrily put it, "In the morning after all the fuss I felt really terrific. I got up and discovered that the goddamn belly no longer existed. I immediately reached down to my knees with my head, something I couldn't do for months, and I tried my arch. It was stretching like rubber, even better than now, because by now I've already overstrained it. At that time the muscles were relaxed but flexible."

At first Makarova was overwhelmed by the sharpness of new feeling.
Even in the hospital she began practicing behind the curtains, bending in
every direction, doing splits. And she would sleep in a rather peculiar position, as she had done in her early childhood, stretching one leg along the
bed while wrapping the other around her head. Like a schoolgirl, she
boasted of her rubber-like elasticity to doctors and visitors. "Look what I
can do," she kept saying, while performing her circus tricks. She terrified
the doctors, and they tried to dissuade her from her gymnastic exaggera-
tions. Suddenly, realizing the consequences of her showing off, she relaxed
for ten days in accordance with doctors' instructions.

After this short period Makarova began taking classes at the San Francisco Ballet School and got on pointe without any hesitation. Her feet were
weak, her calves didn't hold, her stomach muscles gave a lot of trouble,
and she blushed, feeling miserable and helpless, despite the encouraging
comments of colleagues—"Natasha, you're great. You have such courage!"
When in mid-February ABT arrived on tour in San Francisco, Makarova
showed up in class with her "favorite company," dressed all in black,
which merely "underplayed my swellings of a prima donna." To her surprise, the muscles turned flexible "working"; that had never happened in
Russia after her vacations in the Crimea or in the country. When Baryshnikov returned to New York from this ABT tour, he said to me, "Don't worry
about Natalia. She's fine. With a bosom and a rear end, of course, but in
working order."

But his impression was false. On her first day back with ABT she somehow managed to endure class up to the jumps, and the next day she began
with toe shoes on. She teased Miss Chase: "Lucia, would you mind if I do a
pirouette from *Giselle*? Look how simple it is," and the poor lady almost
fainted. The conditioned, though weakened, muscles were demonstrating
the miracle of their natural elasticity. They could contract in a most natural
way—but alas only once. They had to be put on a balletic regimen, forced
to acquire new strength and preserve it. In other words, their natural qualities had to be turned into professional ones.

It was quite a long process. After a month of studying in the private stu-
dio of Janette Sassun in San Francisco, Makarova's muscles began to rebel:
by holding back they refused to contract properly, the back totally lost its
flexibility, the jump disappeared. On the other hand, the turns came out
much better than before, as if for some mysterious reason a new center of
balance had sprung up. Nevertheless, even this little triumph turned out to
be temporary. "I took one step forward and two steps back"—thus Makarova defined that especially distressing period of her professional life.

Her body seemed to need to learn the entire grammar of classical dancing from the very beginning. At first Makarova gave it purely athletic tasks
without any concern for the legato of her movement or the expressiveness of

her dancing. It turned out to be a clever approach: her mechanical technique came back fairly fast. Some movements, such as fouettés, came to her much more easily than before. She even thought her moody body was surrendering to her, but this feeling was premature. As soon as she switched to dancing in her habitual cantilena-like manner, her technique began to limp, disregarding any attempts at control. That experience brought her a little discovery: "By giving my body purely mechanical tasks to perform, I soon acquired technical knacks and strengths akin to those of many good Western ballerinas. I felt myself very equipped and secure. But the legato of dancing totally eluded me. Then the more I oriented myself to the singing quality of my movement, the farther away from me went my virtuosity. Suddenly I came to understand why the Russian bel canto dancing and technical brilliance in the Western sense of the word are almost incompatible. Our cantilena demands that the body be focused on inner, instantaneous muscular responses to the music, whereas mechanical performing based on the counting of measures regards the music as a vehicle for demonstrating physical skill and technical tricks.

"Having realized that, I became very depressed, because I just had to accept my limits and forget about overcoming them. . . ."

At the beginning of April she arrived in New York in an almost hysterical state of mind and said to her private coach, Elena Tchernishova: "I'm falling apart and totally mixed up. One day I'm all right, the next I'm a miserable wreck. I have great hope in you. . . ."

Elena started coaching Makarova five hours a day, sharing with her all the troubles of that time. Makarova's body now was torturing both of them, and sometimes even Elena, usually reserved and patient, was on the brink of despair. When I asked her how she explains this peculiar behavior of Makarova's physical structure, Elena said: "It has nothing to do with the flaws of her training. Her body is utterly conditioned and impeccably maintains an extensive range of classical combinations. But her ability to perform them totally depends on her frame of mind. By nature, Natalia is uneven and intuitive—they say that Anna Pavlova was like this too. The difference is that during her Western period, Pavlova never tackled ballets demanding real virtuosity. She deliberately limited herself to ballets that helped her achieve that delicate balance between technique and its emotional projection. Natalia is in quite a different situation. A number of her ballets demand that she stay in excellent shape. In reacting to certain inconveniences of her life, no matter how slight, her body disobeys her control and starts functioning on its own. It rejects everything imposed on it, including the order of steps. But she never makes the same mistakes twice in class. The only things she has to be careful with are her hips and the small of the back—they have to be watched constantly. That's a juvenile shortcoming overlooked by her tutors at the Vaganova School."

Rehearsing DON QUIXOTE *with Elena Tchernishova*

Dancing is generally a form of escapism as much as a vehicle for achieving a certain balance between outer reality and the inner world of a dancer. The more Makarova is hurt or disturbed by reality, the more passionately she becomes involved in her dancing, attempting to restore her thwarted harmony at the expense of the grammar of classical dance. Subconsciously she relates to this grammar as to something inflicted upon her—another kind of external disturbance. In neo-classical works she feels all right, because the choreographic patterns are less rigid. But the pure classics must be respected as unwritten law, and her body rebels against them for that reason.

During April and May, Makarova was slaving over various ballets she was to perform at the Met during the season: *Other Dances; La Sylphide;* the pas de deux from *Romeo and Juliet* by Igor Tchernishov, revised by Elena Tchernishova; *Voluntaries;* and a brand-new *Don Quixote* staged by Mikhail Baryshnikov after Marius Petipa and Alexander Gorsky. At rehearsals, no matter how uneven they were, I was amazed by one quality of hers that had never made itself felt before: her girlish frailty, so fascinating in her major romantic parts, suddenly yielded to a womanly mature flow, to a seductive pride, to self-assurance. Before, her major charm for me was her touching vulnerability; her plasticity was like that of a dying plant, swaying submissively before death. Now this quality acquired new shadings and overtones: even in the miniature romantic drama of *La Sylphide* this womanly self-assurance helped her portray the ethereal sylvan creature more vividly, with no affectation marring the style. She created an impeccable watercolor figure when dancing, like a violinist using his bow with a minimum of pressure. If earlier she had primarily evoked in my mind the image of Ulanova, now with her attack and self-confident bravura in *Voluntaries* she reminded me of Plisetskaya in her prime. By fighting her still-resisting body, she displayed more vigor, a more explosive vitality. Her gestures became larger and more imperious, and when on June 7 she tackled Kitri for the first time, she danced with an absolutely new flamboyance and hilarious abandon. She seemed to view *Don Quixote* as a vehicle for bravura dancing as much as a dramatic performance of an old vaudeville. Comedy was once Makarova's natural forte. Now she brought this contrived españolade to full life despite the technical flaws and tiny slips that the exhaustion of this cascade of dancing inflicts. Following the patterns of the Kirov, Makarova was not only loyal to the style of this naïve "joke of Petipa's" but managed to create a vivacious character, a Carmen in miniature.

After the Kitri she created at the Met, I lived in anticipation of the *Giselle* that she was scheduled to dance in Philadelphia on June 15.

Makarova's day. . . . On the morning of June 15, I took a cab to pick her up at the house of Mr. and Mrs. Doll in order to catch a train to Philadelphia one hour later. To my surprise, she was still in bed. "Get rid of the cab. . . . I'm not packed yet . . . went to bed at five o'clock this morning. What a person I am—instead of getting enough sleep, I was messing around with my suitcases until dawn. Never know what to take. . . . Decisions, decisions. . . . Will take the next train. Will just arrive for rehearsal. Let's skip class, will warm up by myself. Jesus, how am I supposed to dance tonight? . . . I'm a real wreck!" We got on the next train by a miracle. She instantly fell asleep, rocked by the motion of the train. Suddenly she woke up: "What time? . . . Got to have some coffee. I'm starving. . . . Almost twelve o'clock? In five hours I have to be in the theatre putting on my make-up, warming up, all that stuff. Where am I supposed to dig up the time? Want to sleep like a bear. I'll bomb tonight, remember my words! I don't even know what quality to give my peasant girl this time. Maybe cancel everything to avoid disgrace?" When I reminded her of all the pages she had devoted to interpreting Giselle in this book, Makarova seemed surprised: "Right. One has to do it this way. No overacting, no hysterical fits. That's the point. Simplicity and quiet. In the first act I am concentrated, detached from reality, different from the others. Totally immersed in my inner world . . . like Tatiana in *Eugene Onegin,* but without the French novels. All absorbed in my reveries, in my fantasy Albrecht. Very sensitive and introverted. Otherwise I wouldn't go mad at the first deception of my life.

"Right from the start one has to hold on to this clue. . . ." She was talking with herself, while addressing both me and some invisible opponent.
"In the mad scene there won't be any tossing about, no superfluous frenzy. Everything is very reserved and austere. But in the second act, I must be totally free from my old energy. Must be a sort of all-forgiving spirit. . . . And will love Mischka and absolve him of all sins. . . . Are we arriving? Oh, God, how I want to sleep. . . ."

At three o'clock she showed up at the Sheraton Hotel—frazzled, greyfaced like a ghost. While waiting for her lunch, she instantly got drowsy on the couch. After eating, she went to bed, but in forty minutes we were jolting along in a bus taking us to the theatre. . . .

The theatre disappointed me: open from the sides à la Tanglewood and placing its nine thousand viewers partly on the lawn, it distinguished itself with a circus-like openness that rarely creates the intimate atmosphere necessary for romantic ballet. I wondered how Makarova would subjugate this enormous space to the tribulations of her peasant girl and make them reverberate in the heart of the audience.

As soon as Makarova made her appearance out of her dilapidated hovel (one can't call it anything else, so deplorable is the way it looks in ABT's production) and began her springy jetés around the stage, I felt enormous relief. She had instantly caught the right timing and conveyed the appropriate mood. The audience grew breathless. . . .

That performance was special. I had never seen her dance Giselle with such freedom and simple elegance. From the outset, and throughout the entire ballet, Makarova was not merely an exemplary Giselle in terms of style and romantic technique. She seemed to have found the golden mean in her interpretation. She made the ballet not only an aesthetic joy but a revelation of human experience, magically transfigured by art. She didn't overplay any dramatic moment but executed its combination of steps with so much natural abandon that it might seem as if she were inventing them herself on the stage at that very moment—a kind of artistic freedom reminiscent in a way of Ulanova. Makarova's approach had changed now: from the beginning she made clear Giselle's predestination for death, in whose domain she was to gain her total happiness with Albrecht and demonstrate the power of her love, beyond the grave, outside reality. Thus her Giselle suddenly echoed her Odette. . . .

After the performance she said to me in her dressing room: "You see! Tonight I did exactly what we wrote about *Giselle* in my book. It seemed to work, so even if it never happens again, our writing was worthwhile. . . . But maybe I'm wrong and the performance had nothing at all to do with my analysis of it. Maybe I was simply in a very special mood and felt some kind of inspiration . . . which is precisely the subject we never tackled in the book. And probably we were right not to. Something has to remain unsaid . . . a sort of mystery, to always feed my imagination. If I knew everything about myself as a person, I wouldn't be able to dance. . . . "

—*Gennady Smakov*

Rehearsing DON QUIXOTE

With Anthony Dowell

PHOTOGRAPHIC PLATES

BALLETS

MANON	179
LE SACRE DU PRINTEMPS	192
LES SYLPHIDES	195
VOLUNTARIES	200
LILAC GARDEN	203
SONG OF THE EARTH	206
LE CORSAIRE	209
PILLAR OF FIRE	212
LA SYLPHIDE	214
APOLLO	224
LA BAYADÈRE	227
DARK ELEGIES	234
ROMEO AND JULIET (TUDOR)	237
ROMEO AND JULIET (TCHERNISHOV)	242
ROMEO AND JULIET (MACMILLAN)	244
ELITE SYNCOPATIONS	254
THE NUTCRACKER	256
THE MIRACULOUS MANDARIN	257
THE RIVER	257
CINDERELLA	258
DON QUIXOTE PAS DE DEUX	259
DON QUIXOTE	264
EPILOGUE	266
CONCERTO	267
THE SLEEPING BEAUTY	271
BLUE BIRD PAS DE DEUX	278
AFTERNOON OF A FAUN	280
TCHAIKOVSKY PAS DE DEUX	281
THE FIREBIRD	282
COPPÉLIA	284
CONTREDANCES	292
GISELLE	295
THEME AND VARIATIONS	332
OTHER DANCES	334
LA FILLE MAL GARDÉE	338
ETUDES	343
LES BICHES	344
CHECKMATE	345
EUGENE ONEGIN	346
SWAN LAKE	349
THE DYING SWAN	366

with Anthony Dowell

with Anthony Dowell

with Michael Coleman

with Anthony Dowell

with Anthony Dowell

with Derek Rencher

with Michael Coleman

with David Drew

with Anthony Dowell

LE SACRE DU PRINTEMPS
with Clark Tippet

LES SYLPHIDES
with Ivan Nagy

with Erik Bruhn

with Anthony Dowell; overleaf, with Erik Bruhn 197

VOLUNTARIES
with David Wall

LILAC GARDEN
with John Prinz

with Fernando Bujones

with Gayle Young

SONG OF THE EARTH

with Anthony Dowell and David Wall

with Fernando Bujones

with Ted Kivitt

PILLAR OF FIRE
bottom: with Gayle Young

bottom: with Paolo Bortoluzzi

LA SYLPHIDE
with Ivan Nagy

with Rudolf Nureyev

with Karena Brock and Ivan Nagy

with Ivan Nagy

with Ivan Nagy

with Ivan Nagy

as Gamzatti

as Gamzatti with Oleg Sokolov

with Mikhail Baryshnikov

with Mikhail Baryshnikov

with Mikhail Baryshnikov

DARK ELEGIES

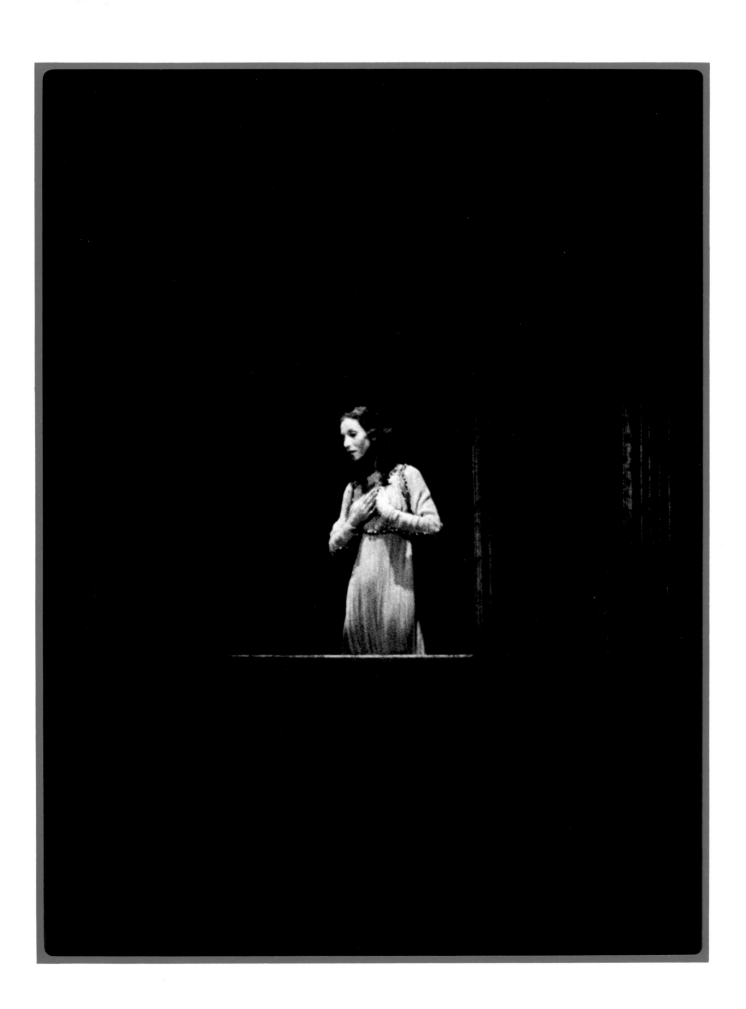

ROMEO AND JULIET (Tudor)

top: with John Prinz

with John Prinz and Martine van Hamel; overleaf, with John Prinz

ROMEO AND JULIET (Tchernishov)

with Ivan Nagy

ROMEO AND JULIET (MacMillan)
with Anthony Dowell

with Anthony Dowell

ELITE SYNCOPATIONS
with Derek Deane

THE NUTCRACKER
(bottom) with Alexander Minz and Mikhail Baryshnikov

THE MIRACULOUS MANDARIN
with Erik Bruhn

THE RIVER
with Erik Bruhn

CINDERELLA
with Anthony Dowell

with Donald MacLeary

with Mikhail Baryshnikov

DON QUIXOTE

EPILOGUE
with Erik Bruhn

CONCERTO
with Ivan Nagy

with Donald MacLeary

with Ivan Nagy

with Mikhail Baryshnikov

with Rudolf Nureyev

with Mikhail Baryshnikov

BLUE BIRD PAS DE DEUX
(THE SLEEPING BEAUTY)
with Fernando Bujones

AFTERNOON OF A FAUN
with Mikhail Baryshnikov

TCHAIKOVSKY PAS DE DEUX
with Patrick Bissell

THE FIREBIRD

COPPÉLIA

with Ted Kivitt

with H. Hysell

with Buddy Balough

with Buddy Balough; overleaf, with Ivan Nagy

CONTREDANCES

with Anthony Dowell

with Yuri Soloviev

with Yuri Soloviev

with Ivan Nagy

with Ivan Nagy

with Mikhail Baryshnikov

with Mikhail Baryshnikov

with Marcos Paredes, Bonnie Mathis,
and Mikhail Baryshnikov

with Vladilen Semenov

with Vladilen Semenov

with Yuri Soloviev

with Erik Bruhn

with Erik Bruhn

with Mikhail Baryshnikov

with Mikhail Baryshnikov

with Mikhail Baryshnikov

with Mikhail Baryshnikov

THEME AND VARIATIONS

with Ted Kivitt

OTHER DANCES

Boyd Staplin at the piano

with Mikhail Baryshnikov

LA FILLE MAL GARDÉE
with Mikhail Baryshnikov

with Mikhail Baryshnikov

with Ivan Nagy

with Enrique Martinez and Ivan Nagy

ETUDES
with Ivan Nagy and Kirk Peterson

LES BICHES

CHECKMATE

EUGENE ONEGIN

with Richard Cragun

SWAN LAKE

with Vladilen Semenov

with Yuri Soloviev

with Sergei Vikulov

with Sergei Vikulov

with Anthony Dowell

with Anthony Dowell

with Rudolf Nureyev

with Anthony Dowell

with Anthony Dowell and Marcos Paredes

with Anthony Dowell

with Ivan Nagy

with Anthony Dowell

with Ivan Nagy

THE DYING SWAN

A NOTE ON THE GRAPHICS

The serif text of this book was set in the film version of Bodoni Book, so called after Giambattista Bodoni (1740–1813), son of a printer of Piedmont. His Manuale Tipografico, *completed by his widow in 1818, contains 279 pages of specimens of types, including alphabets of about thirty languages. His editions of Greek, Latin, Italian, and French classics are celebrated for their typography. In type designing he was an innovator, making his new faces rounder, wider, and lighter, with greater openness and delicacy, and with sharper contrast between the thick and thin lines.*

The sans-serif text is ITC Avant Garde Gothic, which is based on the distinctive logotype used by Avant Garde® Magazine. Both logo and typeface were designed by Herb Lubalin and Tom Carnase. The original drawings have undergone careful refinement to meet the typographic requirements of text and display, yet all weights have retained the refreshing individuality generally referred to as "Avant Garde flavor."

This book was photocomposed by the Clarinda Company, Clarinda, Iowa; the illustrations were printed in two colors by Rapoport Printing Corporation, New York, New York, using their Stonetone Process; and the text was printed in two colors by Halliday Lithograph Corp., West Hanover, Massachusetts. The book was bound by American Book–Stratford Press, Saddle Brook, New Jersey.

R.D. Scudellari directed the graphics and designed the book. Photographic preparation and mechanical art work was done by Joseph Ramer, Assoc. Ellen McNeilly directed the production and manufacturing. Neal T. Jones and Ellen G. Mastromonaco supervised the manuscript and proofs.

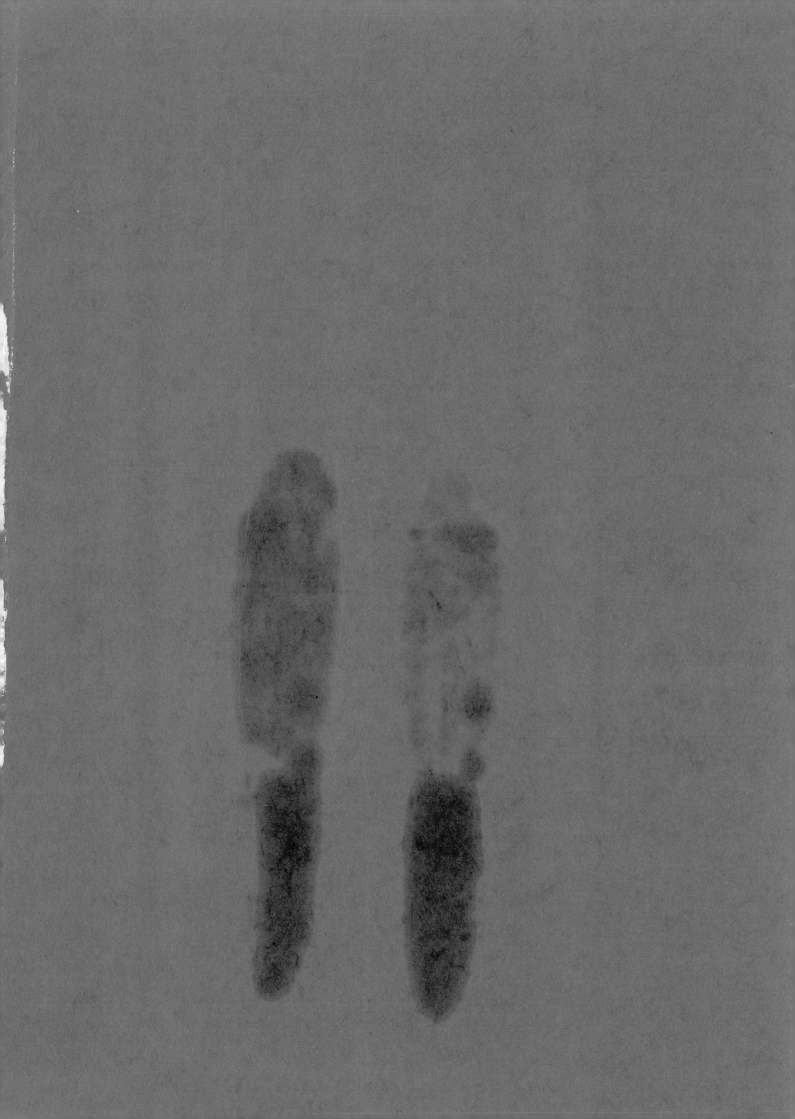

DATE DUE	